lose
weight
now!

lose weight now!

Sara Rose Nicola Graimes Charlotte Watts

p

Notes for readers

Before following any of the advice given in this book we recommend
that you first check with your doctor. Pregnant women, women
planning to become pregnant, children, diabetics, or people with
other medical conditions should always check with their doctor
or health care professional before embarking on any type of diet.
This book is not intended as a substitute for your doctor's or
dietician's advice and support, but should complement the advice
they give you.

This book uses imperial, metric, or US cup measurements. Follow the
same units of measurement throughout; do not mix imperial and
metric. All spoon measurements are level: teaspoons are assumed to
be 5 ml and tablespoons are assumed to be 15 ml. Unless otherwise
stated, milk is assumed to be whole, eggs and individual vegetables
are medium, and pepper is freshly ground black pepper.

The times given for each recipe are an approximate guide only.
Preparation times differ according to the techniques used by different
people and the cooking times may also vary from those
given. Optional ingredients, variations, and serving
suggestions have not been included in the calculations.

This is a Parragon Publishing Book

First published in 2005

Parragon Publishing
Queen Street House
4 Queen Street
Bath BA1 1HE, UK

ISBN: 1-40544-649-8

Printed in China

Designed and produced by
THE BRIDGEWATER BOOK COMPANY

Photographers Clive Bozzard-Hill, Ian Parsons
Home Economist Philippa Vanstone **Thanks to** Karen Heal

contents

introduction

There's no doubt that the western world is in the grip of a weight crisis. If you've picked up a newspaper or turned on the television recently, you can't have failed to notice the headline stories. More than half of the adult population is either overweight or obese and the outlook for our children is even worse. We know we're overweight, which is why dieting is so popular—at any given time, one in three Americans is trying to lose weight. But the sad fact is that 95 percent of dieters put the weight back on, and often end up gaining even more. This book will show you how to break free from the endless cycle of weight gain and dieting for good, and achieve a slimmer, fitter body that you can maintain for life.

Quick fixes—the road to long-term success?

The ultimate goal of any weight control program is a slimmer, trimmer you, but how do you get there? There are hundreds of different diet plans, pills, and magic potions on the market promising maximum weight loss with minimum effort. The truth is that to lose weight and keep it off, you need to make small but significant changes to your eating and activity habits, and make them for good. This book will show you what to do, but you must be prepared to put in time and effort to Lose Weight Now!

How to use this book

It's best to read through the whole book before you start so you've got all the strategies for successful weight loss at your fingertips. You'll find out all about good nutrition and how to eat well for life, as well as what foods it might be wise to avoid. The book is full of practical tips on how to cut calories and stay on track, and there is a range of delicious, inspirational recipes to get you started.

There's also information on exercise, which is essential, not only for weight control, but also for general physical well-being. Some easy, low-impact exercises are described and there's advice on how to keep moving during your everyday life. Finally, a chapter on life after dieting offers top tips on how to stay in control, so that you don't put the weight back on, and stay looking and feeling great.

▶ **Looking good, feeling good**
The right mix of diet and exercise is the only way to ensure that you look and feel your very best.

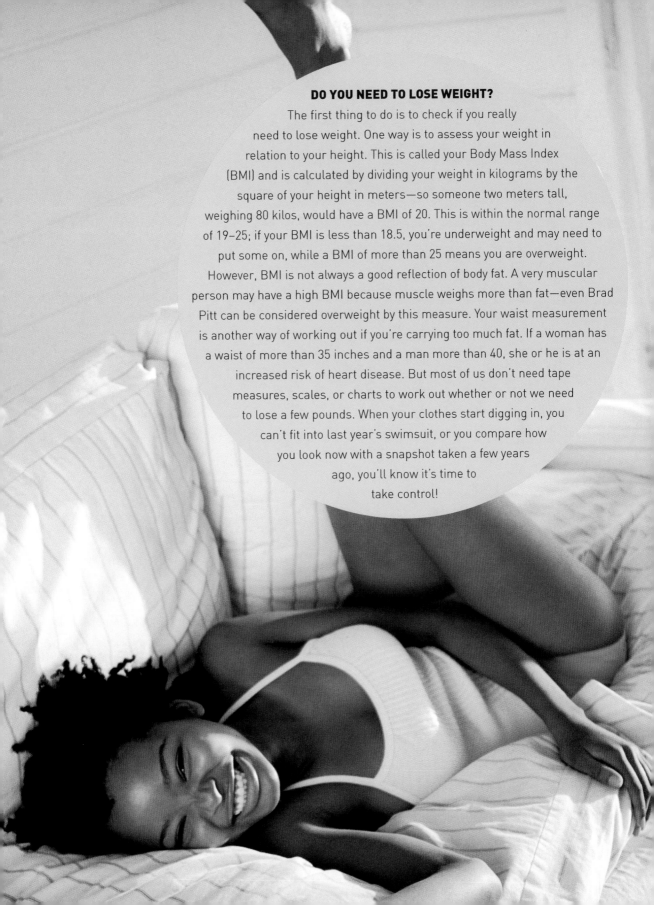

DO YOU NEED TO LOSE WEIGHT?

The first thing to do is to check if you really need to lose weight. One way is to assess your weight in relation to your height. This is called your Body Mass Index (BMI) and is calculated by dividing your weight in kilograms by the square of your height in meters—so someone two meters tall, weighing 80 kilos, would have a BMI of 20. This is within the normal range of 19–25; if your BMI is less than 18.5, you're underweight and may need to put some on, while a BMI of more than 25 means you are overweight. However, BMI is not always a good reflection of body fat. A very muscular person may have a high BMI because muscle weighs more than fat—even Brad Pitt can be considered overweight by this measure. Your waist measurement is another way of working out if you're carrying too much fat. If a woman has a waist of more than 35 inches and a man more than 40, she or he is at an increased risk of heart disease. But most of us don't need tape measures, scales, or charts to work out whether or not we need to lose a few pounds. When your clothes start digging in, you can't fit into last year's swimsuit, or you compare how you look now with a snapshot taken a few years ago, you'll know it's time to take control!

before you start

Diets fail for a number of reasons. These include setting yourself unrealistic goals and feeling you can't meet them; picking a diet that may be too restrictive to follow for any length of time; and trying to lose weight to please other people, rather than yourself. It may also be that you just need to learn a few strategies to help you succeed.

The right frame of mind

First and foremost, have a good think about why you want to lose weight. Make sure you think of benefits that aren't only to do with appearance, such as the alarming statistic that obesity can reduce your life expectancy by up to nine years. Other health benefits of losing weight include being less out of breath, feeling more energetic, and lowering your blood pressure. If you are overweight, losing ten percent of your body weight will have an amazing impact on your general well-being. However, it's absolutely essential that you want to lose weight for yourself, rather than because your partner, family, or friends are nagging you to go on a diet.

Setting realistic goals

If your aim is to turn yourself into Kate Moss, you are probably setting yourself up for failure. Very few people are naturally model-thin. You are far more likely to succeed if you set yourself achievable targets, such as losing eight pounds in ten weeks (the loss of more than a pound a week is not recommended, and weight lost rapidly tends to go back on rapidly). Give yourself a really nice treat (not related to food!) when you have reached this, then set yourself another target. Experts recommend that your diet and exercise goals are SMART— which stands for Specific, Measurable, Achievable, Relevant, and Time-Specific.

▼ **Eat well, keep well**
Eating well should be a pleasure and a delight. A good diet does not have to be a dull diet.

▲ **The wide, wide world**
Take a broad view of the many good reasons to watch your diet—and think about nutrition.

Education

Think of losing weight in terms of starting to play a musical instrument or learning to type. You need to master a set of skills for weight control, including setting realistic goals, choosing and preparing the right foods (you may have to learn new ways of cooking), and maintaining your self-control when everyone around you is trying to tempt you back into bad ways.

Motivation

Your thoughts influence every action, including what you eat and how you perceive yourself. If you always feel that you are depriving yourself while losing weight, it will be very hard to stick to a weight loss routine. However, if you think positively—for example, by recognizing that you feel so much better for eating well and becoming more active—your motivation will remain high. Decide to be someone who can make your aspirations happen, rather than talking yourself into failure. That way, you'll be set for success!

1 all about food

Eating healthily can help you to control your weight—
it is not a quick-fix diet, but rather it will encourage
natural weight loss by showing you the healthiest
way to eat. It is not healthy to lose more than a
pound a week and it is sure, steady weight loss that
ensures that you are burning off fat reserves rather
than muscle. One of the keys to success is to find a
new attitude to food and eating that is not about
"dieting," but about health—giving your body what it
needs, and avoiding what it does not. Food should be
a pleasurable part of life and, if you eat healthily,
there is the added satisfaction of knowing that you
are helping yourself to lose weight.

the truth about diets

Diets have been given much press over the last few years, as weight becomes more and more of an issue and consumption of calorific convenience foods has risen. Some diets claim enormous success, yet many people find them tricky and discouraging. Even if they lose weight initially, they find the pounds piling on again after they stop the regime. Here is a look at some of the most popular diets.

Low-carbohydrate diets

These are very popular, partly because the high meat content appeals to men. They initially allow only ½–2¼ oz (15–60 g) of carbohydrates per day and some vegetables are excluded. People are encouraged to eat proteins and fats such as eggs, meat, and cheese, the principle being that carbohydrates lead to raised insulin levels, under which fat cannot be broken down.

Only fat and protein signal enzymes in the body that let us know when we are full; therefore carbohydrates do not fill us up. Carbohydrates are also broken down and pass through the gut much more quickly, which is why you can be hungry so soon after eating them. This explains why many people on a low-carbohydrate diet end up eating fewer calories, even though fats and proteins have more calories per gram consumed.

Of course, cutting out a major food group can rob you of vitamins and minerals, such as the B vitamins in grains. This can lead to a reduction in energy and therefore less motivation to exercise. Many people also have great difficulty digesting fats and proteins at this level, and high protein foods are acidic, which can lead to liver and kidney problems. Cutting down fiber can also lead to constipation and reduce the elimination of toxins from the bowel.

The reason this diet works for so many people is that they cut out a food to which they have an intolerance, such as wheat. Many

▲ **Be informed**
Always keep up-to-date with the latest information about which foods are healthy.

▶ **The right stuff**
Eat plenty of foods containing vital vitamins and minerals.

people have difficulty digesting wheat and gain weight as a consequence. The diet also helps to keep blood sugar levels steady, which provides energy and reduces food cravings. There are, however, other ways of achieving this, which we shall look at later.

Very low calorie diets

These diets assume that there is a very simple conversion from how many calories you eat to how many you expend through activity. The principle is that if you eat less than the daily required amount of 1950 calories for a woman and 2550 for a man, then you must burn off excess fat. However, if you eat much less than this, the body assumes that you are going through a period when there is little food available, and slows down the metabolic rate to conserve stores. This is why people who go on crash diets can have weight fluctuations. Foods with the same calorific value can also have a completely different effect on weight: the oils in fish, for example, are used up by the brain and therefore there is no excess to be stored as fat. It is "empty calories"—those from foods with little nutritional value—that are the problem. These are stored as fat if not burned off.

Food combining diets

The main goal of food combining diets is to separate your digestion of proteins from your digestion of carbohydrates. People with digestive problems can find these diets very useful, and they have proved successful for weight loss, too. It is not yet wholly understood why this is, though these diets can be tricky to adhere to, and many people simply eat less food as a result. The principle is that different types of food require different enzymes to be broken down in the stomach and small intestine, and there is less work for the body to do if only one set is in operation at a time. Good digestion is an important part of weight loss, as the proper absorption of food and nutrients satisfies the appetite. Constipation can stop the elimination of toxins, which are then reabsorbed, causing the body to hold onto fluids to protect itself. However, protein slows down the release of sugar into the bloodstream, so eating carbohydrates without protein can lead to raised blood sugar levels and sugar being stored as fat.

Low fat diets

Devised on the premise that "all fats are bad," this idea was popular several decades ago, but has since been modified. Weight loss results from avoiding foods that are high in saturated fat, especially those that combine this type of animal-derived fat with sugar. This is why foods like potato chips, pastries, and cookies cause weight gain. However, avoiding all fats starves the body of beneficial fats from fish and plant sources. This can affect hormone balance and the body's ability to regulate fats and cholesterol, both of which can lead to weight gain. Also, many lowfat products replace fats and oils with sugar and additives that can raise blood sugar levels—the main culprit for weight gain.

Points systems

There are many slimming clubs that provide a specific points score for foods based on calorie, fat, and fiber content. A daily limit of points is set and it is up to you which foods you choose. The support group aspect of these clubs works well to motivate people, and sensible, gradual weight loss is encouraged. However, no foods are banned, so some people may use their points up on unhealthy foods, with weight loss occurring simply on account of a lower calorie intake. These people's metabolisms may slow down to conserve energy and they are likely to gain weight after stopping the system. Certain healthy foods may also be avoided because they have high point scores, such as nuts, seeds, and avocados. These foods contain beneficial fats, which is why they have the high scores, but they are vital to a healthy diet.

▲ **Weight for it**
Do not obsess over weighing yourself—once a week is fine. Focus instead on how you are feeling.

Ideal weight ranges

The table below is an indication of acceptable weight ranges for given heights. This is a general guide, which does not take into consideration that muscle weighs more than fat. If you are concerned, consult your doctor to check if your weight is in a risk category, or if you are a good weight for your height and should not lose much if any at all.

HEIGHT–WEIGHT TABLE							
Height		Women			Men		
cm	feet & inches	kg	pounds	stones & pounds	kg	pounds	stones & pounds
152	5′0″	47–62	104–137	7.6–9.11	–	–	–
155	5′1″	48–64	106–140	7.8–10.0	–	–	–
158	5′2″	49–65	108–143	7.10–10.3	58–68	128–150	9.2–10.10
160	5′3″	50–67	111–147	7.13–10.7	59–69	130–153	9.4–10.13
163	5′4″	52–69	114–151	8.2–10.11	60–71	132–156	9.6–11.2
165	5′5″	53–70	117–155	8.5–11.1	61–73	134–160	9.8–11.6
168	5′6″	54–72	120–159	8.8–11.5	62–74	136–164	9.10–11.10
170	5′7″	56–74	123–163	8.11–11.9	63–76	138–168	9.12–12.0
173	5′8″	57–76	126–167	9.0–11.13	64–78	140–172	10.0–12.4
175	5′9″	59–77	129–170	9.3–12.2	64–80	142–176	10.2–12.8
178	5′10″	60–79	132–173	9.6–12.5	65–82	144–180	10.4–12.12
180	5′11″	61–80	135–176	9.9–12.8	66–84	146–184	10.6–13.2
183	6′0″	63–81	138–179	9.12–12.11	68–85	149–188	10.9–13.6
185	6′1″	–	–	–	69–87	152–192	10.12–13.10
188	6′2″	–	–	–	70–89	155–197	11.1–14.1
191	6′3″	–	–	–	72–92	158–202	11.4–14.6

Source: based on Metropolitan Life Insurance Company tables (1983). Note height allows for shoes with 1-inch heels and weight allows for clothing weighing 3 pounds (1.4 kg).

nutrition through life

On the whole, people become less physically active the older they get. This means that their calorific needs are less, and that they should eat less food. It is never a good idea to eat too few calories, however, as eating actually raises the metabolic rate to burn it off as fuel. Skipping meals is a very bad idea, too, as it slows down the metabolism and can cause you to eat more at the next meal. It is true that what you don't burn you can store as fat, but if the food is healthy and nutrient-dense, it will be used up for needs other than fuel, such as structure, brain function, the production of hormones and antibodies, skin healing, neurotransmitters, and as anti-inflammatory agents. Good food, little and often, can keep your body at its most efficient, and will sustain blood sugar levels and energy production. This will keep cravings at bay and encourage exercise.

We all have a basal metabolic rate (BMR), which is the number of calories your body burns each day just to stay alive. Many calorie-burning activities go unseen, such as heart function, detoxification, tissue repair and healing, maintaining the structure of bones and teeth, digestion, and immune function.

Many women find that they put on weight during and after the menopause and become more pear-shaped. This is because of declining estrogen and progesterone levels. It is important to remember that after the ovaries stop producing estrogen, the body's main source of estrogen is fat cells, which emphasizes the importance of including beneficial fats in the diet. Fat cells do not produce progesterone, however, and weight gain on the hips, bottom, and thighs can occur when the ratio of estrogen to progesterone is too high. Increasing exercise and avoiding sugar, refined carbohydrates (like cookies and white bread), stimulants like tea and coffee, as well as reducing meat and dairy intake, and eating more whole foods such as brown rice and beans can help with the removal of excess estrogen and restore balance.

Your relationship with food

For many, eating is a negative coping pattern that suppresses emotions, such as stress, anger, anxiety, boredom, sadness, and loneliness. This comfort eating can begin as a response to a single

▶ **Enjoy your food**
Nothing is more satisfying than eating tasty food that you know is doing you good.

stressful event and eventually becomes a habit that gets you through day-to-day stresses. Unfortunately, it sets up a cycle of eating, not as a response to hunger, but as a distraction from unpleasant feelings.

There is also a physical mechanism at work. When we eat comfort foods, often refined carbohydrates such as chocolate, potato chips, and cookies, we set up a pattern of fluctuating blood sugar levels. This can affect the production of serotonin, the brain chemical that regulates mood. Low serotonin levels can lead to cravings for carbohydrates, a vicious circle that can lead to weight gain. For many, this is worse in the winter, when less sunlight leads to a decrease in natural serotonin. Seasonal Affective Disorder is often linked to weight gain.

Inherited eating patterns

In western society, we tend to swing between continual attempts to diet or eat less in everyday life, and going completely overboard on vacation, at Christmas, and at family events. It is interesting to think that Christmas was originally a feast at which healthy foods were eaten to prepare the immune system for the harshness of the winter ahead. It is certainly not so now.

Big portion sizes, always having dessert, keeping fattening snacks in the house, unhealthy diets, and insisting on finishing an enormous plate of food we do not necessarily want, are all habits learned as children that can follow us into adulthood. These patterns are not set in stone, and establishing a new relationship with food is the first step to making lasting changes.

We must also consider how our eating patterns are shaped by our parents' attitudes to food. Were certain foods withheld, and does this now make you want to eat what you want when you want? Or was food used as a symbol of love and affection that you now associate with comfort and security? If you suspect that your relationship with food is rooted in such psychological issues, then you should seek professional advice to help you break patterns that may be holding you back in achieving your preferred weight.

wholefoods

▲ **Good enough to eat**
How you present your food is just as important as how good it tastes.

optimum nutrition

"Optimum nutrition" means getting the best nutrients possible from your food and avoiding "empty calories." This ensures that your body receives what it needs for all systems to function optimally and for it to manage weight naturally.

MACRONUTRIENTS

These are the larger molecules that provide fuel and structure for your body. It's important to eat sources of these that also provide the most micronutrients, in order to maximize nutritional value.

Carbohydrates

These are made up of glucose molecules that, when digested, break down into sugars that we use as our main source of fuel. If carbohydrates are broken down too quickly, we experience a sharp rise in blood sugar, which is then converted and stored as fat, being dangerous to remain in the bloodstream. Foods that contain these simple sugars are traditionally very sweet, such as fizzy drinks, cakes, cookies, honey, and chocolate. Many people crave these when they get a dip in their blood sugar.

Switching to complex carbohydrates, which take longer to digest, can lead to more sustained blood sugar levels. Good sources of these include the whole grains in brown bread, brown rice, oats and rye, vegetables, beans, and darker fruits such as berries, plums, and cherries, and crisp, green apples, which all release their sugars slowly. These foods also provide fiber, which cleans out toxins, and have plenty of nutrients that are crucial to weight loss. Limit your intake of very sweet fruits like grapes and bananas, and of fruit juice, which is very high in sugar.

▼ **Bake your own**
The less processed your food, the more you know about its ingredients.

Proteins

These form the structures in our organs, antibodies, hormones, and neurotransmitters. We can also burn proteins for fuel, if absolutely necessary, although there is a risk that you will also burn muscle. Proteins are very good for blood sugar management and can slow down the release of sugar into the bloodstream when eaten with carbohydrates. They can also speed up metabolism, but should be eaten within reasonable limits to avoid excess acidity, which encourages weight gain. They are a good breakfast food as they ensure sustained energy throughout the day. Meat, fish, and eggs provide the densest sources, but proteins are also found in brown rice, beans, nuts, seeds, and dense vegetables like broccoli and asparagus. Generally, proteins should make up 30 percent of your daily calorie intake.

Fats

These are essential to make steroid hormones, HDL cholesterol ("good" cholesterol), and all cell membranes. Fats also make up the majority of our brains. Saturated fats are generally found in animal products, and although we can handle them in small amounts, they can offset beneficial fats and lead to weight gain when eaten with carbohydrates. Oils are generally beneficial when not overprocessed (avoid hydrogenated fats or oils). Oily fish (salmon, mackerel, tuna, and sardines) contain omega-3 oils, which help the body to produce serotonin. Nuts, seeds, and their oils contain omega-6 oils, which help to regulate blood sugar. Monounsaturated oils are found in nuts, peanuts, avocados, and olives, and their oils; they contain oleic acid, which helps to regulate cholesterol and helps the body to deal with fats.

MICRONUTRIENTS

As the name suggests, these are smaller, but no way less important than macronutrients. We shall look at those that are termed essential, which means that we must eat them every day because we cannot make them in our bodies.

Vitamins

These are chemicals that enable enzyme reactions to happen in your body. They are separated into two categories:

Water-soluble vitamins are not easily stored and we need to eat them often: at least 500 mg of vitamin C is needed daily. It is vital for hormone production and the clearance from the liver of toxins that can add to weight gain. Good sources are berries, citrus fruits, and vegetables, especially broccoli, bell peppers, and asparagus.

▲ **Be fruitful**
Make sure you eat at at least five portions of fruit or veg each day.

B vitamins are important for weight loss and are lost in foods that are processed. They enable us to produce energy, regulate mood, and deal with stress. They are found in meat, fish, whole grains, vegetables, and beans.

The fat-soluble vitamins are transported around the body in oils and fats, and work in fatty areas like the heart, liver, skin, and eyes, where they protect the organ from damage. They include vitamin A, vitamin E, and the carotenoids, and are found in brightly colored fruit and vegetables, nuts, seeds, and fish.

Minerals

Every living cell on the planet depends on minerals from the rocks that make up the earth and get into our systems via the soil. Poor mineral status is a common underlying cause of weight gain.

Bulk minerals are needed in large amounts, most notably calcium and magnesium (from green leafy vegetables, nuts, seeds, and fish), which work closely together in the body and regulate heart function, fluid balance, and muscular activity. Trace minerals are needed in smaller amounts, but are still essential. Particularly important for weight loss is zinc, which has the most uses in the body, including blood sugar balance and serotonin production, and is found in nuts, seeds, fish, beans, and legumes.

Antioxidants

These are the vitamins A, C, and E, the carotenoids and the minerals zinc and selenium (found in Brazil nuts, seafood, and whole grains). They are important in the weight loss process, protecting the body as you burn off fat. There are also natural plant chemicals with antioxidant properties, such as the cyanidins found in red, blue, and purple fruits, and lycopene, which is found in tomatoes, watermelon, and pink grapefruit.

The greater the variety of fruits and vegetables that you eat, the more nutrients you will receive. The World Health Organization recommends at least five portions a day. One portion is roughly a palmful, one whole larger fruit or several small ones such as plums. It is best to meet this target with raw fruits and vegetables, and to limit the intake of fruit juice, diluting this where feasible.

▼ Variety is the spice of life
The more varied and colorful your choice of fruit and veg, the more nutrients you will be eating.

water and the importance of fluids

Your body's makeup is 70 percent water and it likes to stay that way. Vast amounts of water are used daily to maintain most of your bodily functions and to get toxins completely out of your body, rather than being reabsorbed and recirculated. Signs of dehydration include dry skin, headaches, constipation and hard stools, poor concentration, and bloating. As with weight gain, if the body feels "starved" of water, then it will hold onto the little it has, which can lead to water retention.

Water is lost through the bowels, urine, and sweat and needs to be continually replaced. The average requirement is eight glasses a day. You can also help to make this up with noncaffeinated teas and diluted fruit juices. Like everything, balance is important and there is a level at which anything becomes toxic. Drinking five times this amount of water has been shown to be dangerous.

If you are very dehydrated, build up your water intake slowly or you can shock the body. Diluting apple juice with the same amount of water can help to get water into your cells, but be careful not to drink too much as it is high in sugar.

Water is important for weight loss as it promotes the removal of toxins and acts as a temperature regulator. It assists in the function of enzymes and proteins, which work better diluted, and helps the body to reach its optimum fat-burning function.

Caffeine

Caffeine, found in coffee, tea, cocoa, chocolate, green tea, and cola drinks, is dehydrating. This is because it has a toxic effect on the nervous system, and the body uses up water when eliminating it through the kidneys. It is also a diuretic, meaning that it causes excess urination and water loss. Any caffeine you drink increases your need for water to replace what is lost. Caffeine is counterproductive in weight loss because it is a stimulant, causing epinephrine to be produced, with a subsequent rise in blood sugar.

A large coffee bought in a café can have as much as several hundred milligrams of caffeine, while a brewed filter coffee may contain 100 mg. A cup of tea made with a tea bag has an average of 40 mg, but of course this depends on how long it is brewed. Green tea can be very useful for helping to reduce and give up caffeine. It contains just 4 mg per cup (even decaf tea contains 3 mg) but, unlike black tea, does not overstimulate. That small amount of caffeine can be enough to ward off your craving, which is unfortunately a sign of caffeine withdrawal. Weaning yourself off caffeine completely takes three days of avoidance, but be prepared for side effects and stick with it.

Alcohol

Alcohol should be completely avoided on the 14-day diet plan (see page 26). It contains calories with no nutritional value and depletes the body of B vitamins, vitamin C, magnesium, and zinc, thus making blood sugar control more difficult. Alcohol is also loaded with sugar. This causes an immediate stimulatory action, although it is ultimately a depressive drug. Like sugar, alcohol can be rapidly turned to fat by insulin, the hormone responsible for blood sugar control. This fat is deposited in the body and stored in the liver, which it may damage. When blood sugar levels are low, alcohol is often used to raise them, setting off another vicious circle. The ethanol that causes intoxication is toxic to the body and damages all the liver's detoxification pathways. Good liver function—achieved through a "clean" diet, with plenty of fiber and little or no sugar—is crucial to weight loss.

◀ **Water for life**
Always keep some water handy and make a note of how much you are drinking.

a diet that works

get ready to lose weight

This 14-day diet plan is an example of a healthy eating regime that is designed to allow you to make long-lasting changes and lose weight naturally, steadily, and safely. It is not about seeking a quick fix, but about realizing what makes you feel better about your body and health to motivate you to form new habits.

The foods mentioned in this chapter are pantry essentials, so you are always prepared to eat something healthy. Organization helps you to set up healthy eating patterns and is satisfying in itself. The 14-day diet plan is carefully constructed to provide you with a nutrient-rich diet containing the ideal amount of calories, following the principles of healthy eating set out in this book.

the 14-day program

"Breakfast like a king, lunch like a prince, and dine like a pauper" is the best rule to live by when it comes to maintaining energy levels. It also encourages natural weight loss because you use up your energy more efficiently during the day. At breakfast, including a protein source can maintain blood sugar balance by providing a sustainable energy source; this can help to reduce cravings. Porridge oats are an alternative quick, easy breakfast. Try to make lunch your main meal of the day when possible and eat dinner no later than 7:30 p.m.

Snacking keeps your blood sugar steady, as long the snack is something like fruit, raw almonds, vegetable sticks, hummus, or sesame seed paste. Plain yogurts with real fruit are good, as are smoothies if they have no added sugar and especially if they contain dark fruits or berries. Try a taste test with healthy snack bars and buy those with the least sugar. Radishes are a good snack as they improve thyroid function, which helps weight loss.

The amount and variety of vegetables most people eat are sadly lacking. Find ways to eat vegetables that appeal to you. Herbs, spices, olive oil, lemon juice, sunflower, pepitas, and sesame seeds, horseradish sauce, whole grain mustard, soy sauce, pesto, and sesame seed paste all add flavor. If you have had a sweet palate for years, then changing that to appreciate the taste of vegetables, herbs, and spices can take time, but will gradually happen as you wean yourself off sugar. Eating zinc foods such as nuts, seeds, and fish can help increase your sense of taste.

How to follow the program

Firstly, read the program thoroughly and make a list of foods that you will need to buy. Sticking to a diet always involves forward planning and this also makes you feel more in control. If you are particularly busy on one day and find the plan difficult, do not feel guilty for deviating, but get back on track as soon as you are able. You can swap a day that seems to fit in with your schedule better and use examples of ingredients to make informed, healthier choices when eating out or buying something preprepared because of time restraints.

Try to set aside time to do the diet so that you are not fighting against it and feeling frustrated. Concentrating on looking after yourself and making important changes in your life should be given time and priority, especially getting used to new habits, shopping choices, and foods. You will find out over the 14 days which recipes suit your lifestyle and tastes. Learn to listen to your body and note what it reacts to (in good and bad ways) to gain an understanding of how best to continue after the 14 days are finished. You may want to repeat the diet, especially if you feel more reassured when you have specific dietary guidelines to follow.

If you fall off the wagon, do not be too harsh on yourself, but take the opportunity to note how, although the foods you were tempted by made you feel better in the short term, their effect was negative in the long term.

Carb-curbing

Some people find that they have more success if they limit their intake of starchy carbohydrates such as rice, pasta, and bread in the evening because it is more likely to be stored as fat if not used for energy. The 14-day diet only includes small portions of carbohydrate in the evening, or none at all. Replace with bulky vegetables such as broccoli and cauliflower. Raw almonds are good for stopping carb cravings, as are foods high in tryptophan (from which serotonin is produced), such as poultry, oily fish (buy in cans for snacks on rye crackers), oatcakes, nuts, and seeds.

▲ **Get organized**
Planning your meals helps you to feel in control and meet your goals.

◀ **Big breakfast**
Cereals release energy slowly during the day and limit cravings.

the program

The following is a 14-day diary outlining recipes in this book, other meal suggestions and snacks to start you on the road to natural, healthy weight loss. It is best to start on a Saturday so you have the weekend to get used to the changes and shop for foods. You can have the breakfast in already and then spend Saturday morning making up your shopping list and buying in the other foods. Recipes included in this book are highlighted in capital letters.

Day One—Saturday

Breakfast Poached eggs on rye bread—can add spinach to make eggs Florentine.

Lunch TABBOULEH.

Dinner GRIDDLED VENISON WITH ORANGE SALSA—have as many vegetables as you can to start your new habit of using them to fill you up.

Snack DETOX JUICE—have this midmorning or after shopping, and always drink fresh.

Day Two—Sunday

Breakfast Poached eggs, broiled, lean organic bacon, and tomato—a healthy alternative to the fried breakfast.

Lunch CARROT & RED LENTIL SOUP—soups can be made at the weekend and stored or even frozen for midweek lunches and snacks.

Dinner Try a less calorific roast dinner without the roast potatoes and parsnips, which release their sugars very quickly and contain lots of fat and carbs—the worst combination. Choose a lean chicken breast with plenty of veg and boil just a few new potatoes in their skins.

Snack STRAWBERRY & PEACH SMOOTHIE—a Sunday afternoon treat that will satisfy any sweet cravings.

▼ **Sweet treat**
A Strawberry & Peach Smoothie in the afternoon is a relaxing treat.

Day Three—Monday

Breakfast Always have breakfast. If you are usually rushed, just get up 15 minutes earlier. Find a nonprocessed, good quality whole grain cereal that you like. If you suffer from digestive or skin problems, headaches, or bloating, decrease or avoid wheat and see if this helps.

Lunch THAI CHICKEN BROTH.

Dinner GLAZED SALMON FILLET WITH ASPARAGUS or TERIYAKI TOFU & VEGETABLE STIR-FRY.

Snack Snack on raw almonds to beat any sugar cravings, especially those that have you reaching for sweet foods or caffeine around 4 p.m.

Day Four—Tuesday

Breakfast Variety is important at breakfast to ensure you get a full spread of nutrients and do not encourage food intolerances. Try porridge for some days during the week, with different toppings such as berries (which can be added directly to the hot porridge from the frozen packages found in supermarkets), raw nuts, and seeds. Do not sweeten with sugar, but apple juice or a small amount of honey is fine.

Lunch Make a salad with boiled eggs, capers, green beans, and a large leafy salad pack. These packs are always useful for making a quick meal and can even be snacked on like a bag of potato chips— you will be surprised at how much energy green foods can give you!

Dinner ITALIAN BEAN & PASTA SOUP—if you have eaten a big lunch and kept up your blood sugar during the day by snacking on healthy foods, then it is easier to have dinner "like a pauper."

Snack STRAWBERRY & PEACH SMOOTHIE.

▲ **Keep it simple**
Healthy and attractive meals can be easy to prepare.

Day Five—Wednesday

Breakfast Try a different breakfast cereal, and add a topping, like one of the porridge toppings mentioned for Day Four, or some plain yogurt.

Lunch FRESH TUNA NIÇOISE—get used to making this classic quickly or preparing it for work the night before as it travels well. You can play around with the ingredients for variety.

Dinner PASTA WITH ITALIAN MEATBALLS IN TOMATO SAUCE— again, try to eat no later than 7:30 p.m., especially as this meal contains pasta. A tempting vegetarian alternative is the MUSHROOM, BEAN, & SPINACH TOWER.

Snack Always keep apples with you as a fantastic, energy-releasing food that will satisfy your sweet palate. They also help rid the body of toxins that can keep the body holding onto weight.

Day Six—Thursday

Breakfast Fresh fruit salad will give you a refreshing start to the day.

Lunch ROASTED RED ONION, AVOCADO, & SPINACH SALAD—if you need, you can add some cold brown basmati rice as a good source of complex carbohydrates, B vitamins and fiber to keep you going through the day.

Dinner ASIAN FISH PACKAGES.

Snack Try raw radishes.

Day Seven—Friday

Breakfast Choice of any from last week.

Lunch Make up a salad with canned sardines or mackerel, avocado, lettuce, watercress, and your favorite other salad items. Grated carrot and zucchini make refreshing salad-bulkers.

▲ **Menu for change**
Ringing the changes with a range of exciting dishes helps to keep you motivated.

Dinner CHILI CHICKEN WITH CHICKPEA MASH—a tasty treat that can be shared with friends at a dinner party.
Snack Children's fruit bar or health bar (check sugar content).

Day Eight—Saturday
Breakfast Smoked mackerel or haddock with poached eggs and rye bread.
Lunch SESAME SHRIMP NOODLE SALAD.
Dinner TABBOULEH—good to keep as a snack, it can always be added as a side dish to meals with fish, meat, or tofu.
Snack DETOX JUICE—get used to making this so that it becomes part of your weekly routine.

Day Nine—Sunday
Breakfast DETOX JUICE—it's good to start the day with a cleanse when you have time (can be done in the week too). Have a handful of nuts and seeds as well to provide protein and slow down sugar release from the juiced fruits.
Lunch Try having the roast dinner (see last week) at lunchtime so you have more time to burn off calories. You do not have to have meat; a piece of fish, or a whole baked trout can be just as satisfying. Keep some aside to make a salad with tomorrow.
Dinner TERIYAKI TOFU & VEGETABLE STIR-FRY—light and quick for a relaxing Sunday evening.
Snack STRAWBERRY & PEACH SMOOTHIE.

Day Ten—Monday
Breakfast Try things other than milk to go with your cereal, such as plain yogurt, unsweetened soy, oat, or rice milk.
Lunch Use the extra meat, fish,

▼ **That's entertainment**
These healthy meals are perfect for dinner parties.

▲ **Pep up your veg**
Vegetables can be more exciting
and varied than you might think.

or chicken you cooked on Sunday to put together a salad.
Add some canned artichokes or sun-dried tomatoes.
Dinner SESAME SHRIMP NOODLE SALAD.
Snack Boiled eggs make great, transportable snacks.

Day Eleven—Tuesday
Breakfast Fresh fruit salad.
Lunch ROASTED RED ONION, AVOCADO, & SPINACH SALAD—with brown
rice or rye bread, if needed.
Dinner SEAFOOD SKEWERS WITH ARUGULA SALAD.
Snack Crudités—slice vegetables such as celery, cucumber, red
bell pepper, and carrot.

Day Twelve—Wednesday
Breakfast Choice of any from last week.

Lunch FRESH TUNA NIÇOISE.

Dinner TURKEY KOFTAS WITH LEMON COUSCOUS
or LASAGNA WITH ROASTED VEGETABLES.

Snack Keep reaching for those apples.

Day Thirteen—Thursday

Breakfast Choice of any from last week.

Lunch GLAZED SALMON FILLET WITH ASPARAGUS.

Dinner BAKED LEMON HADDOCK WITH CHUNKY SALSA
or TERIYAKI TOFU & VEGETABLE STIR-FRY.

Snack Choose from the variety of healthy snacks that you should
now be used to having to hand.

Day Fourteen—Friday

Breakfast Think about which is your favorite and most practical
breakfast because you will invariably gravitate toward this more
often. Still try to have variety, though, and a bigger breakfast when
you have time.

Lunch Make a salad of your choice with as many of your favorite
salad items as possible so that you really enjoy it.

Dinner Treat yourself to a Friday night takeout—
choosing is the key here. Thai food is light, and
has plenty of spices, garlic, and ginger that
are good for weight loss. Avoid anything
deep-fried, but opt instead for a clear
soup, fish, chicken, or shrimp with
vegetables and a little steamed rice.
Splash out—the better the restaurant,
the less oily and fresher the
ingredients will be.

Snack Have a little treat to
congratulate yourself on all your hard
work. A small bar of semisweet
chocolate will provide satisfaction and
also the beneficial properties of cocoa
without the problematic milk solids and too
much sugar. Denying yourself everything can take
the joy out of life, so the occasional weekly treat is
good for you and keeps the willpower up.

▼ **Just reward**
An occasional treat helps to keep
that vital motivation going.

exercise and looking after your body

Regular exercise is essential for successful weight loss because physical activity boosts your metabolic rate and calorie-burning muscle mass. As you become older, your metabolism slows down and your body uses up fewer calories, so you need to remain active throughout life to avoid the pounds creeping on. However, getting fit doesn't happen overnight. You have to commit yourself to making exercise part of your life. Most of us know that regular exercise is an essential part of a healthy lifestyle, but still the majority of us does far too little. Research has shown that exercise protects health, prolongs life, and can reduce the risk of disease. It also builds up your flexibility, stamina, and strength. When you exercise regularly, you not only change your physical appearance, you also experience a greater sense of mental and emotional well-being. It should also help you sleep better, feel less stressed, and more in control of your life. So what are you waiting for? It's time to get moving.

all about exercise

Half the battle with exercise is getting started in the first place and then keeping it up on a regular basis, but there are plenty of good reasons to keep you going. Both your body and your mind benefit from physical activity. When you exercise, your brain releases chemicals called endorphins that make you feel relaxed and in a better mood. Exercise can help with depression, and the feeling of well-being that follows exercise also reduces stress and tension.

The physical benefits of activity are tremendous. If you exercise regularly, your heart muscles become stronger and are able to pump blood more efficiently. As a result, blood pressure is lowered and cholesterol levels reduced as the blood flows more quickly around the body, picking up fatty deposits and waste products, reducing your risk of developing heart disease or having a stroke. The lungs also become stronger and your body more efficient at using oxygen. Joint mobility and stability are improved, which can help to keep you independent and active in later life. Bones stay strong and healthy, and muscles become stronger.

Different types of exercise

Any type of activity that gives the heart and lungs a good workout is known as aerobic activity. Types of aerobic exercise include swimming, dancing, skating, running, cycling, soccer, rowing, and racket sports. Just as important for fitness are flexibility and strength. Flexibility exercises (stretching) make your joints and muscles more supple; strength exercises such as weightlifting make your muscles stronger, help reduce body fat, and make your body appear more toned. Strength and flexibility make you less likely to injure yourself when going about your daily activities or when exercising.

Getting started

To start exercising, choose an exercise you enjoy, because you are much more likely to do it regularly. Plan when you are going to do it—scheduling exercise helps you to continue. It's great to start exercising when you're on a diet, but if you want to keep the weight off you're going to have to stay active in the long term.

Experts recommend that we should spend half an hour exercising at least five times a week. They all agree that little and often is effective, which may suit you better than a more structured workout. As you become fitter, you can increase the amount of exercise you do and the time you spend doing it. Always be aware of how your body feels during and after exercise. Build up gradually, especially if you have not exercised for a while.

Caution

Consult your doctor if you have not exercised for several years, if you are very overweight, if you are pregnant, if you are over 45 years of age, if you have a history of high blood pressure or high cholesterol, or if you have heart or lung disease or any long-standing medical condition. Certain types of exercise may not be appropriate for you.

DON'T PANIC!

Exercise tones and builds muscle, which actually weighs more than fat. As you become fitter, your weight may increase slightly. However, muscles burn up more calories than fat, so this weight shouldn't stay on for long if you're watching what you eat. It's important to remember that you are becoming fitter, not fatter. Exercise also increases your appetite so you need to be very careful to resist eating too much.

◀ **Look after your body**
Regular exercise will help you lose weight and keep it off.

how to fit exercise into your day

Most of us complain that we simply don't have the time to exercise regularly, but exercising doesn't have to mean heading off to the gym five times a week for a grueling workout. The key words are little and often—just 10 minutes one or two times a day can make a significant impact on your fitness levels. Attack the housework with vigor, walk or cycle to work if you can, garden with a vengeance, get intimate with your partner, or just dance around the kitchen to your favorite tunes. And try to spend some of your leisure time being active—a long walk after Sunday lunch will benefit all the family.

Perfect posture

If your posture is good, you'll look thinner and taller. Notice how when you lift your chin up and pull in your stomach muscles you feel trimmer and more confident. The trick is to make this second nature. Not only will you look better, but you will also benefit physically. Good posture keeps the body in its correct position, reduces the strain on your back, and allows the internal organs to function efficiently. Poor posture stops you breathing properly, strains muscles and ligaments, and over time can push your body out of shape. Joint inflammation, pain, and stiffness may also develop.

Good posture looks natural and relaxed, not slouched or hunched. When standing, your neck should be in line with your spine with your head balanced squarely on top, your shoulder blades set back and down and your spine long and naturally curving. Stand with your feet hip-width apart. Gently pull up through your legs, keeping your knees slightly bent. Lengthen your spine, pull in your stomach muscles, and stand tall. Keep your shoulders down and relaxed so that your neck is as long as possible. Perfect posture takes practice, but when you've mastered the technique you'll reap the benefits.

▲ **Clean up and shape up**
Vacuum cleaning, ironing—even dusting—will all help to improve your fitness level.

**HOW TO BURN CALORIES
WITHOUT EVEN REALIZING IT**

Exercise is not just something you do at the gym—it's an integral part of your everyday life. If you'd rather have your teeth pulled than go to an exercise class, take comfort from the fact that exercise doesn't have to be hard or boring. Just look for ways to use energy and you can greatly increase the amount of exercise you take. Start by simply hiding the TV's remote control! Get off the bus one stop farther from home, walk up and down escalators, wash your car by hand instead of using the carwash, use a basket rather than a cart in the supermarket. The possibilities are endless.

The right equipment and clothing

Proper shoes are key to preventing strains and sprains. Invest in a decent pair of trainers appropriate to your chosen sport— specialist sports stores should be able to advise you. Wear loose, comfortable clothing so that your skin can breathe and so that your movements won't be restricted. If you are exercising outside, wear layers of clothes that can be removed as you warm up.

take a deep breath

Breathing is something you do automatically, but it can be consciously controlled. It's well known that if you're feeling agitated, taking a deep breath will calm you down. Unfortunately, years of stress and poor lifestyle means shallow, rapid breathing is the norm for most of us, whereby we use only the top third of our lungs. If you don't breathe properly you will restrict your oxygen supply and raise your blood pressure. Correct breathing comes from the deepest area of the lungs and benefits both your body and mind. You'll benefit from a lower heart rate, reduced blood pressure, and lower levels of stress hormones. Breathing properly is essential when you're exercising—the rule is to breathe in just before you make a movement and breathe out with each effort.

The right frame of mind

Positive thinking will motivate you to start an exercise program, keep you on track, and even work out more effectively. A positive mental attitude helps you to succeed because it does not allow thoughts of failure. One way to become more positive is to repeat statements (affirmations) to keep you on track, such as "I am becoming fit and healthy" or "Exercise is great and I can feel the benefits already." Repeat your personal mantras several times a day or write them down and stick them where you will see them—on a mirror or on the refrigerator door. Soon you will start to believe them.

Mind over matter

Visualization is a technique that uses the imagination to help you fulfill your potential. It is commonly used by athletes in preparation

HOW TO BREATHE DEEPLY

The following exercise, known as abdominal breathing, will help you breathe more deeply, but it can be quite difficult to master. Here the diaphragm, the sheet of muscle forming the top of the abdomen, is used to help the lungs inflate and deflate without effort. You may feel a little dizzy when you start to do this—it's because you're taking in more oxygen than you're used to.

1 Sit comfortably. Put one hand on your chest and the other just below the breastbone. Breathe in slowly through your nose.

2 Hold the breath for a few seconds, then breathe out slowly through your mouth. Expel as much air as you can.

3 Repeat three or four times. Try to concentrate on your breathing as you do this rather than anything else.

▲ The power of nature
Visualizing a favorite place can help you to achieve a positive frame of mind.

for competition. Motivation can be boosted by mentally rehearsing the sequence of events required for a successful performance. According to the theory, if visualization is repeated enough, expectations rise and you begin to act as if the image were a reality. So you can use visualization to keep up with your exercise program, envisaging your slimline, toned body, and also as a means of sticking to a sensible eating program, envisaging the weight dropping off. Anyone can visualize, though it may take a little practice. Just find a quiet place, lie down or sit in a comfortable chair, and close your eyes. Breathe slowly and try to relax before focusing on your chosen mental image.

basic body workouts

Try to get used to doing some body exercises once a day. The following pages show you exercises to shape up and slim down your body. It's up to you how many you do—as you become fitter, you can build up the amount. Start by doing at least five of each, unless otherwise instructed, and make sure your movements are slow and controlled.

Warming up and cooling down

Always follow a routine to stretch your muscles, tendons, and ligaments before and after exercising. This makes you less likely to injure yourself and helps avoid muscle strain and stiffness. Warming up should involve aerobic exercise such as jogging on the spot for a few minutes followed by a series of stretches. Unless otherwise instructed, repeat the stretches on both sides of your body, and try to hold each stretch for at least five seconds.

◀ Whole body stretch

1 Stand tall, arms by your side, and feet slightly apart.
2 Raise your arms straight above your head.
3 Clasp your hands together. Now stretch your arms up as high as you can. You will feel the stretch in your arms, chest, abdomen, hips, and thighs. Repeat three times.

▲ Torso-twister

1 Sit on the floor with one leg straight and the other bent and crossed over it.
2 Turn toward the bent knee, place the opposite arm in front of the knee, and push against that leg while turning your body toward your other arm.

▶ Hip and thigh stretch

1 Kneel with one knee directly above its ankle and stretch the other leg back so that the knee touches the floor.

2 Place your hands on your front knee to stabilize yourself.

▶ Side stretch

1 Stand up straight with your feet shoulder-width apart.

2 Put one arm over your head, lean from the waist, and reach slowly to the side with your upper hand.

upper body

Say goodbye to unsightly bat wing arms with these fabulous firming exercises!
They'll also sculpt your torso.

▼ Hands, arms, and shoulders

1 Stand tall with your feet slightly apart. With your upper
arms against your body, bunch your fists at shoulder level.
2 Stretch up with your right arm, spreading your fingers
as wide as possible.

3 Look up at your hand and
stretch for a count of five. Clench
your fist again and return to the
starting position.
4 Repeat with your left arm.
5 Now stretch up with both arms, spreading your fingers wide.
Look up at the ceiling and stretch for a count of five.
Return with clenched fists to the starting position.

KEEP YOUR FLUIDS UP
When you exercise, fluids are
lost as you sweat and as you
breathe out. To keep yourself
hydrated, drink a glass of water
before you start exercising and one
after you have finished, even if
you don't feel thirsty.

▶ Dips

1 Before starting this exercise, place a chair
against a wall.
2 Stand with your back to the chair, bend
your legs, and grasp the seat of the chair.
3 With your bottom raised and your back
straight, slowly bend your elbows to about
90 degrees as you lower your
bottom toward the floor.
4 Straighten your arms to
return to the starting point.

▶ Arms, shoulders, and sides

1 Stand with your feet hip-width apart.

2 Clasp your hands above your head, palms upward, and stretch toward the ceiling.

3 From your waist, bend to the right, keeping your arms stretched.

4 Return to the center and bend to your left.

▶ Arm and chest muscles

1 Stand tall with your feet slightly apart, arms straight out to the sides at shoulder level, palms facing upward.

2 Make small circles with your arms, increasing to large circles. Return to small circles.

stomach and waist

Keeping your stomach muscles trim is key to preventing lower back pain and enabling you to perform arm and leg exercises safely and efficiently. We tend to store extra fat around our waists, and you'll get a firmer, flatter midriff by working the abdominal muscles correctly and regularly.

▼ Basic stomach trimmer

1 Lie on your back. Pull your knees in toward your chest.
2 Thrust your legs straight out at an upward angle, hold for a count of ten, then slowly lower your legs to the floor.

▶ Waist twists

1 Stand with your feet hip-width apart and knees slightly bent.
2 Tighten your abdominal muscles.
3 Hold your arms out in front of you, bent at an angle as if you were a hula dancer.
4 Twist your shoulders and head around to one side, then return to the center, keeping your hips still as you do so. Repeat on the other side of your body.

▲ Advanced stomach trimmer

1 Lie on your back with your feet hip-width apart and your feet firmly on the floor. Keep your knees bent.
2 Rest your hands on your thighs.
3 Use your stomach muscles to lift your shoulders gently off the floor, then lower.
4 Your back should remain in contact with the floor at all times.
5 To make this exercise even more difficult, cross your hands over your chest.

▶ Side bends

1 Stand with your feet hip-width apart, knees slightly bent.
2 Tighten your stomach muscles and slide one hand down the side of your leg.
3 Return to the center and repeat on the other side.

lower body exercises

Who wants a sagging bottom or wobbly thighs? Practice these exercises for lissom legs and buttocks of steel!

▼ **Inner thigh muscles**

1 Lie on your back, legs straight up, feet pointing toward the ceiling.

2 Bend your knees and imagine you are a frog. Slowly spread your legs out to the sides as far as possible.

3 Return to the starting position.

◀ Hips and thighs

1 Lie on your back, knees bent, arms out to the sides.

2 Keeping your knees together, swing them over to the left, until your left leg touches the floor.

3 Make sure both shoulders stay flat on the floor. Then repeat on your right side. Repeat ten times each side.

◀ Legs

1 Lie on your left side, with your head supported by your left forearm, with your legs together, and your right hand on the floor in front of you for support.

2 Keep your hips facing forward and your body in a straight line.

3 Bend both knees back. Gently raise the top leg, then lower it. Repeat ten times, tensing your buttock as you raise and lower your leg.

4 Repeat on your right side with your left leg.

◀ Buttocks

1 Sit on the floor, legs straight in front of you, and arms folded across your chest.

2 "Walk" on your buttocks—ten steps forward, ten steps back.

facial workout

Muscles have to be exercised to stay firm and fit and this applies to your face just as much as to your body. Facial muscles are different from the rest of the body in that they are directly attached to the skin that covers them. When the facial muscles droop, so does the skin attached to them. Practice the following exercises two times a day to retain your youthful looks and keep your face as toned and fit as your body.

For the sitting exercises, sit in front of a mirror so that you can make sure you are exercising properly. Keep your back teeth together, lips slightly apart, and try not to squint or tense your eye muscles.

▶ Cheeks

1 Grin as widely as you can and hold for a count of five. Repeat twice.
2 Snarl upward using the muscles on either side of your nose and hold for a count of five. Repeat twice.
3 Assume a relaxed smile with your lips closed, then suck your cheeks onto your teeth. Hold for a count of ten. Repeat ten times.

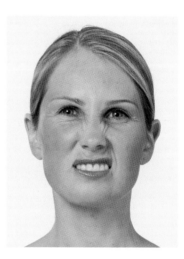

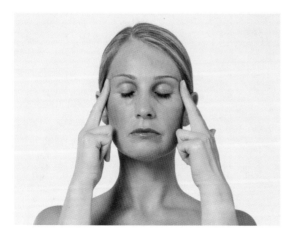

◀ Eyes

1 Press two fingers on either side of your head at the temples while opening and closing your eyes rapidly. Repeat five times.
2 Sit upright with your eyes closed. While keeping your eyes closed, look up then down as far as possible. Repeat ten times.
3 Sit upright, looking straight ahead with your eyes open. Look up then down while keeping your head still. Repeat ten times, then look left, then right. Repeat ten times.

▶ Neck and chin

1 Slap lightly under your chin with the back of your hand about 30 times in quick succession.

2 Sit up straight, tilt your head back, and look at the ceiling while keeping your mouth closed. Start to chew slowly. Repeat 20 times.

3 Jut your chin forward and very slightly upward. Place your lower lip over your top lip. Slowly smile up and out. Hold for a count of five, gently stroking upward with the back of your hand along your jaw line. You should feel a good pull around your jaw line and throat. Gradually release your lip hold and relax. Repeat five times.

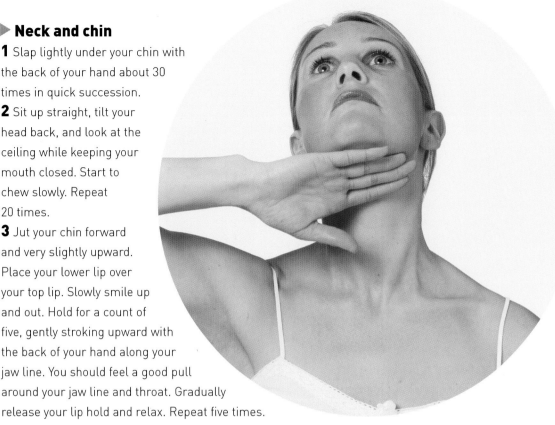

◀ Forehead

1 This exercise can be done seated, standing, or lying down facing the ceiling. Lift your eyebrows as high as possible, opening your eyes very wide. Relax and repeat ten times.

2 Using your fingers, lightly stroke from the bridge of your nose on each side of your face up and out along your forehead to your hairline. Repeat five times.

3 Place the pads of your fingertips along your hairline. Push upward gently and hold the skin against the bone. Look straight ahead. Now try to bring your brow down against the resistance of your hold, closing your eyes gradually. Hold this downward pull for a count of three, then slowly relax. Repeat three times.

skin care

At first glance, information about skin care may not seem to have much place in your program to lose weight. However, one of the results of not eating properly or exercising is that our bodies become loaded with toxins that may then be converted into an unsightly substance called cellulite. This is an accumulation of fat, fluid, and toxins that have become trapped in the deeper layers of your skin, giving it a lumpy, dimpled appearance. Most women, even if they are very slim, have some cellulite because they are genetically programed to store fat, but excess weight makes it look much worse.

Beauty experts believe that a daily and weekly body care routine, which can easily be carried out at home, will increase the elimination of toxins, helping you to get rid of fat. Specific body treatments, from exfoliation to skin brushing, will leave you feeling pampered and will significantly improve the appearance of your skin and the efficiency of your body's elimination processes.

Skin brushing

Skin is your body's largest organ, losing about 1 lb 2 oz/0.5 kg of waste products every day through its pores. Skin brushing helps clear the pores and makes your skin glow. It also improves blood and lymph circulation, helping to relieve water retention and enabling the more efficient removal of waste products from the cells.

How to brush your skin

Use a loofah, a dry flannel, a dry, rough towel, or a long-handled, natural bristle brush. Always brush your skin when dry, not wet, and never brush the face as the skin here is very delicate. Follow the sequence below and spend about five minutes a day brushing

▲ **Water power**
A blast of cold water after a hot shower can help to perk up your circulation.

your skin. Strokes should be long and firm and made in the direction of your heart.

1 Brush both sides of your feet and up your legs.

2 Brush over your chest and toward the heart. Using gentle, circular strokes, brush your stomach in a clockwise direction.

3 Raise each arm and brush along from your hand to your armpit.

4 To finish, brush from your bottom up your back to your neck as far as you can reach.

Exfoliation

This describes the process of removing dead skin cells. It gives your skin a deep clean, helping it to get rid of impurities, and should be done once a week. Relax in a warm bath tub for 10 minutes, then rub your body all over with an exfoliating scrub—you can buy one or make your own. Pay particular attention to areas of rough skin and rub as hard as is comfortable. Wash the exfoliant off in the bath, then get out and gently pat yourself dry. Apply a body oil or thick moisturizer to help keep your skin soft and retain moisture.

▲ **Deep clean**
Regular exfoliation will improve your skin's appearance.

Showering

Every day, a hot shower followed by a blast of cold water will do wonders for your skin and circulation. Alternate 3 minutes of hot water and 1 minute of cold water, at least once, for maximum results.

4 recipes

This collection of recipes has been created with taste, variety, and health in mind. You are guaranteed not to feel deprived with our cleansing juices, hearty soups, substantial salads and lowfat meat and fish dishes, not forgetting impressive vegetarian options. Many of the recipes are also low in carbohydrates and gluten-free, and where fats are included, they are usually the healthier ones, such as the omega-3 fatty acids found in oily fish. The emphasis is on fresh produce that provides a wide range of vitamins, minerals, and fiber—the ingredients for good health.

detox juice

This morning energizer contains beet, one of the most effective liver-cleansing vegetables.

2 eating apples

½ cup white seedless grapes

1 large carrot

2 oz/55 g cooked beet in natural juices

½ inch/1 cm piece of fresh gingerroot

Preparation time 5 minutes **Serves 1**

1 Quarter the apples, then put them through a juicer along with the grapes, carrot, beet, and ginger. Serve at once.

One serving contains:

Energy kCal 394.25

Protein g 3.42

Carbohydrate g 99.53

Sugars g 78.95 **Fat g** 2.51

Saturates g 0.52

Fiber g 16.08 (before juicing—most lost in process)

Sodium g 0.07

strawberry and peach smoothie

Try to use natural live plain yogurt when making this smoothie as it contains beneficial bacteria that are good for the digestive system. If peaches are out of season, you could try bananas instead.

1 peach

140 g/5 oz strawberries

250 ml/9 fl oz natural live plain yogurt

One serving contains:
Energy kCal 269.04
Protein g 12.53
Carbohydrate g 35.6
Sugars g 29.94 **Fat g** 7.93
Saturates g 1.97
Fiber g 3.91
Sodium g 1.56

Preparation time 5 minutes **Serves 1**

1 Peel and pit the peach, then coarsely chop. Hull the strawberries and halve if large. Put the fruit into a blender with the yogurt and blend until smooth and creamy. Serve at once.

italian bean and pasta soup

This classic minestrone-style soup is hearty enough to be eaten as a meal in itself.

1½ tbsp olive oil

1 onion, diced

1 celery stalk, thinly sliced

1 large carrot, coarsely chopped

1 bay leaf

1 tsp dried oregano

6 cups vegetable stock

1¾ cups strained canned tomatoes

6 oz/175 g dried pasta shapes, such as penne or conchiglie

9 oz/250 g canned cannellini beans, drained and rinsed

4½ cups fresh spinach leaves, tough stalks removed

½ cup Parmesan cheese shavings (optional)

salt and pepper

One serving contains:
Energy kCal 349.30
Protein g 15.29
Carbohydrate g 53.72
Sugars g 5.46 **Fat g** 8.97
Saturates g 1.66
Fiber g 6.97
Sodium g 1.12

Preparation time 10 minutes

Cooking time 30 minutes **Serves 4**

1 Heat the olive oil in a large, heavy-bottom pan. Add the onion and cook, covered, over medium-low heat for 8 minutes until softened. Add the celery, carrot, and bay leaf and cook, stirring occasionally, for an additional 3 minutes.

2 Add the oregano, stock, and tomatoes and bring to a boil. Reduce the heat, cover, and let simmer for 5 minutes.

3 Stir in the pasta and beans, bring back to a rolling boil, and cook for about 10 minutes, uncovered, until the pasta is tender but still al dente. Stir occasionally to prevent the pasta sticking.

4 Add the spinach and cook for an additional 2 minutes or until the spinach has wilted. Season with salt and pepper to taste and divide the soup between 4 bowls. Sprinkle with the Parmesan just before serving.

carrot and red lentil soup

This thick, nutritious soup is a good source of vitamins, minerals, and fiber. Serve with seeded whole wheat rolls as a light meal.

1½ tbsp olive oil

1 large onion, chopped

1 celery stalk, chopped

4 carrots, chopped

1 cup split red lentils, rinsed

2 fresh rosemary sprigs, each about 4 inches/10 cm in length

1 bay leaf

6 cups vegetable stock

salt and pepper

Preparation time 15 minutes

Cooking time 45 minutes **Serves 4**

1 Heat the oil in a large heavy-bottom pan. Add the onion, cover the pan, and cook for 8 minutes over medium-low heat until softened. Add the celery and carrots, then cook for an additional 3 minutes, stirring occasionally.

2 Add the lentils, rosemary, bay leaf, and stock, then bring to a boil. Reduce the heat and let simmer, half-covered, for 30 minutes or until the lentils are very soft. Occasionally skim off any foam that rises to the surface while cooking the lentils.

3 Remove the rosemary sprigs and bay leaf, then transfer the soup to a blender or use a hand-held blender. Blend the soup until smooth. Return the soup to the pan, season with salt and pepper, and reheat if necessary.

One serving contains:
Energy kCal 264.36
Protein g 13.63
Carbohydrate g 40.22
Sugars g 6.95 **Fat g** 4.04
Saturates g 0.23
Fiber g 0.16
Sodium g 8.13

thai chicken broth

This light, lowfat soup is packed with flavor. You could serve it with egg or rice noodles for a more substantial light meal.

scant 7¼ cups chicken stock

2 stalks of lemon grass, peeled, halved lengthwise, and crushed with the back of a knife

6 slices of fresh gingerroot, plus 4 slices peeled and cut into short thin sticks

4 kaffir lime leaves

4 tsp Thai fish sauce

4 skinless, boneless chicken breasts, about 5 oz/140 g each

3 garlic cloves, thinly sliced

scant 2¼ cups fresh spinach leaves, tough stalks removed

3 tbsp rice vinegar

2 tbsp lime juice

2 Thai chilies, seeded and finely chopped

salt and pepper

2 tbsp chopped fresh cilantro

Preparation time 15 minutes

Cooking time 25 minutes **Serves 4**

1 Place the chicken stock, lemon grass, 6 ginger slices, lime leaves, and fish sauce in a large pan. Add the chicken breasts and bring to a boil. Reduce the heat and let simmer, half-covered, for 20 minutes.

2 Remove the chicken and set aside, then strain the stock, discarding the solids.

3 Return the stock to the pan and add the ginger sticks, garlic, spinach, rice vinegar, lime juice, and chilies and let simmer for 2–3 minutes.

4 Slice the chicken into strips and divide between 4 bowls. Pour over the soup. Season with salt and pepper, if necessary, and garnish each serving with fresh cilantro.

One serving contains:

Energy kCal 186.33

Protein g 34.06

Carbohydrate g 5.28

Sugars g 1.82 **Fat g** 1.98

Saturates g 0.49

Fiber g 0.98

Sodium g 0.34

tabbouleh

You could use couscous instead of bulgur wheat to make this refreshing, filling salad. To transform it into a light meal, top with slices of grilled provolone cheese. Tabbouleh is best served at room temperature.

generous 1 cup bulgur wheat

2 cups boiling water

8 vine-ripened tomatoes, seeded and chopped

3 inch/7.5 cm piece of cucumber, diced

3 scallions, finely chopped

4 tbsp chopped fresh mint

4 tbsp chopped fresh cilantro

4 tbsp chopped fresh parsley

8 slices of provolone cheese (optional)

DRESSING

juice of ½ lemon

2 tbsp extra virgin olive oil

salt and pepper

Preparation time 15 minutes

Cooking time 3 minutes, plus 25 minutes soaking **Serves 4**

One serving contains:
Energy kCal 336.09
Protein g 9.01
Carbohydrate g 59.09
Sugars g 11.39 **Fat g** 8.91
Saturates g 1.19
Fiber g 12.5
Sodium g 0.04

1 Cover the bulgur wheat with the boiling water in a large bowl. Stir and let stand for about 20–25 minutes or until the bulgur is tender but still retains some bite. Drain well.

2 Transfer to a serving bowl and let cool slightly. Add the tomatoes, cucumber, and scallions and toss until combined. Stir in the herbs.

3 Mix together the lemon juice and olive oil to make the dressing and pour it over the salad. Mix well with a spoon, then season with salt and pepper to taste.

4 If serving with the provolone, heat a stovetop grill pan until hot. Place the provolone on the pan and cook for about 2–3 minutes, turning halfway. Serve the provolone on top of the tabbouleh.

sesame shrimp noodle salad

This Japanese-style salad makes a complete meal for two people or serves four as an appetizer. Instead of the shrimp, you could try slices of broiled chicken or marinated tofu.

9 oz/250 g rice noodles

1 carrot, sliced into fine julienne (short, thin) strips

2 inch/5 cm piece of cucumber, seeded and finely sliced into thin strips

4 scallions, thinly sliced on the diagonal

4 tomatoes, seeded and diced

1 hot fresh red chili, seeded and finely sliced into circles

8 oz/225 g cooked jumbo shrimp

1 tbsp sesame seeds, lightly toasted

2 tbsp chopped fresh cilantro

salt and pepper

DRESSING

1 tsp grated fresh gingerroot

1 garlic clove, crushed

4 tsp soy sauce

1 tbsp sesame oil

1 tbsp light olive oil

1 tbsp lime juice

Preparation time 15 minutes

Cooking time 5 minutes **Serves 2–4**

1 Cook the noodles in salted boiling water following the package instructions. Drain and refresh under cold running water.

2 To make the dressing, mix together the ginger, garlic, soy sauce, sesame oil, olive oil, and lime juice until combined.

3 Place the cooked noodles in a large serving bowl and add the carrot, cucumber, scallions, tomatoes, and chili. Pour over the dressing and mix together until thoroughly combined. Season to taste with salt and pepper.

4 Divide the noodle salad between 2–4 plates, top each serving with some shrimp, then sprinkle with sesame seeds and fresh cilantro before serving.

One serving contains:
Energy kCal 570.67
Protein g 19.29
Carbohydrate g 94.72
Sugars g 7.60 **Fat g** 12.44
Saturates g 1.08
Fiber g 5.19
Sodium g 0.95

fresh tuna niçoise

This main course salad is a healthy twist on the classic French dish. Serve it with crusty whole wheat bread.

10 oz/280 g small new potatoes, scrubbed

6 oz/175 g fine green beans, trimmed

7 oz/200 g romaine lettuce, leaves separated and torn into bite-size pieces

generous 1 cup watercress

1 small red onion, thinly sliced

12 cherry tomatoes, halved

½ cup black olives

olive oil, for brushing

juice of ½ lemon

4 tuna steaks, about 4 oz/115 g each

1 tbsp chopped fresh flat-leaf parsley

salt and pepper

DRESSING

1 tbsp extra virgin olive oil

1 tsp white wine vinegar

3 tbsp reduced-fat mayonnaise

1 small garlic clove, crushed

Preparation time 15 minutes

Cooking time 20 minutes **Serves 4**

One serving contains:
Energy kCal 354.93
Protein g 30.20
Carbohydrate g 19.06
Sugars g 5.36 **Fat g** 17.13
Saturates g 2.27
Fiber g 3.81
Sodium g 0.45

1 Steam the potatoes and green beans until tender, using separate pans. Drain the potatoes and let cool. Refresh the green beans under cold running water and let cool.

2 Place the potatoes and green beans in a large serving bowl with the salad greens, onion, tomatoes, and olives.

3 Blend together the ingredients for the dressing and spoon it over the salad. Season with salt and pepper and toss the salad with your hands until all the ingredients are coated.

4 Brush a stovetop grill pan with some olive oil and heat until very hot. Squeeze the lemon juice over the tuna and season, then cook the fish for 4–5 minutes, turning once, until golden outside but slightly pink in the center. Sprinkle with parsley, season with salt and pepper, and serve at once with the salad.

roasted red onion, avocado, and spinach salad

This simple salad makes a good accompaniment to any broiled meat, chicken, or fish dish. Roasting the onions first tempers their fiery flavor and adds a delicious sweetness to the salad.

1 large red onion, peeled and cut into 8 wedges

olive oil, for oiling roasting pan

5 cups fresh baby spinach leaves, tough stalks removed

1 large avocado, pitted, peeled, and cut into bite-size pieces

1 tsp lemon juice

DRESSING

juice of ½ lemon

3 tbsp extra virgin olive oil

½ tsp Dijon mustard

salt and pepper

Preparation time 10 minutes
Cooking time 25 minutes **Serves 4**

One serving contains:
Energy kCal 222.37
Protein g 3.03
Carbohydrate g 16.56
Sugars g 3.21 **Fat g** 17.35
Saturates g 2.85
Fiber g 7.39
Sodium g 0.10

1 Preheat the oven to 400°F/200°C. Place the onion wedges in a lightly oiled roasting pan and cook for about 25 minutes, turning occasionally, until tender and golden at the edges. Remove from the oven and let cool.

2 Place the spinach leaves in a serving bowl. Toss the avocado in the lemon juice to prevent it browning and add it to the spinach with the onion.

3 To make the dressing, whisk the lemon juice into the oil, then stir in the mustard. Alternatively, you could place the dressing ingredients in a screw-top jar and shake until combined. Season the dressing and pour it over the salad. Serve at once.

chili chicken with chickpea mash

These chicken breasts are coated in a vibrant chili paste called harissa, which adds flavor and keeps the chicken moist. Serve with green beans and broccoli.

4 skinless chicken breasts, about 5 oz/140 g each

1 tbsp olive oil

8 tsp harissa (chili) paste

salt and black pepper

CHICKPEA MASH

2 tbsp olive oil

2–3 garlic cloves, crushed

14 oz/400 g no salt or sugar canned chickpeas, drained and rinsed

4 tbsp semiskim milk

3 tbsp chopped fresh cilantro

One serving contains:
Energy kCal 473.79
Protein g 34.79
Carbohydrate g 27.35
Sugars g 7.43 **Fat g** 24.90
Saturates g 4.03
Fiber g 4.47
Sodium g 0.72

Preparation time 15 minutes plus 30 minutes marinating
Cooking time 30 minutes **Serves 4**

1 Make shallow cuts in each chicken breast. Place the chicken in a dish, brush with the olive oil, and coat both sides of each breast with the harissa paste. Season well with salt and pepper, cover the dish with foil, and let marinate in the refrigerator for 30 minutes.

2 Preheat the oven to 425°F/220°C. Transfer the chicken breasts to a roasting pan and roast for about 20–30 minutes until they are cooked through and there is no trace of pink in the center.

3 Meanwhile make the chickpea mash. Heat the oil in a pan and gently fry the garlic for 1 minute, then add the chickpeas and milk and heat through for a few minutes. Transfer to a blender or food processor and purée until smooth. Season to taste with salt and pepper and stir in the fresh cilantro.

4 To serve, divide the chickpea mash between 4 serving plates, top each one with a chicken breast, and garnish with cilantro.

griddled venison with orange salsa

Venison is low in fat compared with other types of red meat. Here, it is served with a flavorful orange salsa. You could also accompany it with boiled new potatoes and a mixed green salad.

ORANGE SALSA

2 oranges, peeled, segmented and diced

2 shallots, diced

juice and finely grated rind of 2 limes

1–2 hot fresh chilies, finely chopped

2 tbsp extra virgin olive oil

6 tbsp chopped fresh mint

salt and pepper

olive oil, for brushing

4 venison steaks, about 4½ oz/ 125 g each

salt and pepper

One serving contains:
Energy kCal 356.86
Protein g 40.13
Carbohydrate g 11.66
Sugars g 7.78 **Fat g** 16.63
Saturates g 3.34
Fiber g 2.10
Sodium g 0.07

Preparation time 10 minutes
Cooking time 10 minutes **Serves 4**

1 To make the salsa, place the orange, shallots, lime juice and rind, chili, olive oil, and mint in a bowl. Season to taste with salt and pepper and mix well. Set aside to allow the flavors to merge.

2 Brush a stovetop grill pan with oil and heat until smoking. Season the venison and cook for 4–5 minutes on each side.

3 Serve each venison steak with 2 large spoonfuls of salsa.

pasta with italian meatballs

These meatballs are cooked in a rich tomato sauce to keep them moist and succulent, and to avoid having to use extra oil. Serve with a green salad.

1¾ cups lean ground pork

1 onion, grated

2 tsp dried oregano

2 garlic cloves, crushed

1 small egg, beaten

salt and pepper

10½ oz/300 g dried whole wheat spaghetti

fresh basil leaves, to garnish (optional)

TOMATO SAUCE

1 tbsp olive oil

2 garlic cloves, chopped

generous 1 cup dry white wine

2½ cups strained canned tomatoes

1 bay leaf

2 tsp sun-dried tomato paste

Preparation time 20 minutes, plus 30 minutes chilling
Cooking time 30 minutes **Serves 4**

1 Place the ground pork, onion, oregano, garlic, and egg in a bowl and mix until combined. Season with salt and pepper, cover the bowl with plastic wrap and let chill for 30 minutes.

2 Meanwhile, make the tomato sauce by heating the olive oil in a large sauté pan and frying the garlic over low heat for 1 minute. Increase the heat, pour in the white wine, and boil until the wine has reduced and the smell of alcohol has disappeared. Reduce the heat to medium-low, add the strained tomatoes, bay leaf, and tomato paste, stir, and cook, half-covered, for 5 minutes.

3 Remove the meatball mixture from the refrigerator and form it into walnut-size balls. Place the meatballs in the tomato sauce and cook, half-covered, over medium-low heat for 15–20 minutes until they are cooked through.

4 Meanwhile, cook the pasta in boiling salted water following the package instructions until al dente. Divide between 4 shallow bowls and top with the meatball sauce, garnished with basil.

One serving contains:
Energy kCal 662.14
Protein g 31.74
Carbohydrate g 69.06
Sugars g 7.25 **Fat g** 26.80
Saturates g 8.36
Fiber g 2.75
Sodium g 0.72

turkey koftas with lemon couscous

Lamb is more often used to make koftas but turkey is lower in fat and makes the perfect foil for the aromatic herbs and spices.

1 lb 2 oz/500 g ground turkey

1 large onion, finely chopped

2 tbsp chopped fresh cilantro

2 tbsp chopped fresh parsley

1 tsp ground coriander

½ tsp chili powder

1–2 tbsp olive oil

salt and pepper

LEMON COUSCOUS

generous 1½ cups couscous

1 tsp bouillon powder

4 tbsp lemon juice

4 tbsp chopped fresh cilantro, plus extra to garnish

salt and pepper

One serving contains:
Energy kCal 517.36
Protein g 31.65
Carbohydrate g 59.51
Sugars g 4.19 **Fat g** 16.47
Saturates g 2.92
Fiber g 4.58
Sodium g 0.38

Preparation time 25 minutes
Cooking time 30 minutes **Serves 4**

1 Place the turkey, onion, herbs, ground coriander, chili powder, and salt and pepper seasoning in a food processor, then blend.

2 Divide the mixture into 12 portions and, using wet hands, shape each one around a skewer (soak wooden skewers in water first for 15 minutes, to prevent burning). Let chill for 30 minutes.

3 Heat a stovetop grill pan or skillet and add half the oil. Cook the skewers in 2 or 3 batches, adding oil if necessary and turning occasionally, for 10 minutes or until browned and cooked through.

4 Meanwhile, make the lemon couscous. Place the couscous in a bowl and pour in enough boiling water to cover by ½ inch/1 cm. Stir in the bouillon powder. Let stand for about 5 minutes until the water has been absorbed, then fluff up with a fork. Stir in the lemon juice and fresh cilantro. Season with salt and pepper.

5 Serve 3 skewers per person and accompany with the lemon couscous. Garnish with extra cilantro, if liked.

asian fish packages

Cooking the fish in a package helps it to retain its moisture and absorb the flavors of the accompanying ingredients. It also helps to seal in nutrients.

4 thick cod fillets, each about 7 oz/200 g

1 garlic clove, thinly sliced

4 thin slices of fresh gingerroot, peeled and cut into short thin sticks

4 baby leeks, cut into thin strips

2 small carrots, cut into thin strips

½ red bell pepper, seeded and cut into thin strips

4 tbsp lime juice

4 tsp light soy sauce

2 tbsp fresh apple juice

1 tsp sesame oil

salt and pepper

fresh cilantro, to garnish

Preparation time 15 minutes

Cooking time 20 minutes **Serves 4**

One serving contains:

Energy kCal 231.65

Protein g 37.38

Carbohydrate g 13.39

Sugars g 5.92 **Fat g** 2.77

Saturates g 0.30

Fiber g 1.98

Sodium g 0.31

1 Preheat the oven to 400°F/200°C. Place each cod fillet on a piece of foil or parchment paper that is large enough to make a package. Arrange some garlic, ginger, leeks, carrots, and bell pepper on top of the pieces of fish.

2 Mix together the lime juice, soy sauce, apple juice, and sesame oil, then spoon the mixture over the fish. Season with salt and pepper, then fold the foil or paper to make a loose package.

3 Place the packages on a baking sheet and bake for 15–20 minutes, depending on the thickness of the fillets, until the fish is cooked. Carefully open each package and transfer the fish and its toppings to 4 plates. Garnish with cilantro before serving.

baked lemon haddock with chunky salsa

The tomato and herb salsa adds plenty of oomph to the simply cooked plain fish. Serve with steamed zucchini and broccoli.

4 thick haddock or cod fillets, about 7 oz/200 g each

olive oil, for brushing

8 thin slices of lemon

salt and pepper

2 tbsp olive oil

1 garlic clove, crushed

3 tbsp chopped fresh parsley

3 tbsp chopped fresh basil

juice of 1 lemon

SALSA

8 vine-ripened tomatoes, seeded and diced

2 shallots, diced

One serving contains:
Energy kCal 231.65
Protein g 37.38
Carbohydrate g 13.39
Sugars g 5.92 **Fat g** 2.77
Saturates g 0.30
Fiber g 1.98
Sodium g 0.31

Preparation time 15 minutes
Cooking time 20 minutes **Serves 4**

1 Preheat the oven to 400°F/200°C. Rinse and dry each haddock fillet and place on a piece of foil that is large enough to cover the fish and make a package.

2 Brush each fillet with a little olive oil and top with two slices of lemon, then season with salt and pepper. Fold over the foil to encase the fish. Place the packages in a roasting pan and bake for 15–20 minutes or until just cooked and opaque.

3 Meanwhile, to make the salsa, place the tomatoes, shallots, olive oil, garlic, parsley, basil, and lemon juice in a bowl. Mix until combined and season to taste with salt and pepper.

4 Carefully unfold each package and arrange the fish and its juices on 4 serving plates. Place a spoonful of salsa by the side.

glazed salmon fillet with asparagus

The marinade adds a rich golden glaze to the salmon. You could steam the asparagus instead of grilling it, if preferred.

MARINADE

2 garlic cloves, crushed

1 tsp grated fresh gingerroot

4 tbsp fresh apple juice

2 tsp maple syrup

2 tbsp soy sauce

1 tsp sunflower-seed or corn oil

salt and pepper

4 salmon fillets, about 4½ oz/140 g each

olive oil, for brushing

20 asparagus spears, trimmed

1 tbsp sesame seeds, lightly toasted

Preparation time 15 minutes, plus 1 hour marinating

Cooking time 10 minutes **Serves 4**

One serving contains:
Energy kCal 320.77
Protein g 31.13
Carbohydrate g 8.76
Sugars g 5.69 **Fat g** 17.56
Saturates g 3.38
Fiber g 2.07
Sodium g 0.54

1 Mix together all the ingredients for the marinade and season with salt and pepper. Place the salmon in a shallow dish and pour the marinade over, turning the fish to ensure it is coated. Cover with plastic wrap and let marinate in the refrigerator for at least 1 hour, turning the fish occasionally.

2 Preheat the broiler to high. Line the broiler pan with foil and place the salmon on top. Spoon half of the marinade over the fish and broil for about 6 minutes, turning once, until just cooked but still pink in the center.

3 Meanwhile, heat a stovetop grill pan pan and brush it with some olive oil. Arrange the asparagus in the pan and cook for 3–4 minutes until just tender.

4 Place the remaining marinade in a small pan and bring to boil. Arrange the asparagus on 4 plates, then top each one with the salmon. Spoon the marinade over the fish and sprinkle with the sesame seeds. Serve at once.

seafood skewers with arugula salad

These simple sweet chili marinated kabobs can be barbecued instead of broiled, if preferred. They are served with a lightly dressed arugula salad.

4 tbsp sweet chili sauce

2 tbsp hot water

2 garlic cloves, crushed

1 inch/2.5 cm piece of fresh gingerroot, peeled and grated

½ tsp crushed dried chilies

juice and rind of 2 limes

16 raw jumbo shrimp, shelled and deveined

8 oz/225 g salmon, skinned and cut into large bite-size pieces

12 oz/350 g firm white fish, skinned and cut into large bite-size pieces

salt and pepper

lime wedges, to serve

ARUGULA SALAD

scant 2¼ cups arugula leaves

1 tbsp olive oil

1 tsp lemon juice

salt

One serving contains:
Energy kCal 268.12
Protein g 33.42
Carbohydrate g 8.73
Sugars g 4.74 **Fat g** 10.71
Saturates g 1.46
Fiber g 0.60
Sodium g 0.63

Preparation time 15 minutes, plus 30 minutes marinating
Cooking time 5 minutes **Serves 4**

1 Mix together the sweet chili sauce, hot water, garlic, ginger, chilies, and lime juice and rind in a shallow dish. Add the shrimp, salmon, and white fish to the dish and turn to coat them in the marinade. Season to taste with salt and pepper. Cover with plastic wrap and let marinate for 30 minutes in the refrigerator.

2 Preheat the broiler to high and line the pan with foil. Divide the fish and shrimp between 8 skewers, starting and finishing each one with a shrimp.

3 Arrange the skewers in the broiler pan and spoon over half the marinade. Broil for 2 minutes, turn and spoon over the rest of the marinade and broil for an additional 2–3 minutes. Place 2 skewers on each plate and pour over any marinade left in the pan.

4 To make the arugula salad, toss the arugula leaves in the olive oil and lemon juice and season with salt. Serve with the skewers and lime wedges.

mushroom, bean, and spinach tower

This impressive looking dish makes a perfect dinner party main course served with new potatoes and a salad.

2 tbsp olive oil, plus extra for brushing

8 large portobello mushrooms

4 tbsp water

1 zucchini, sliced lengthwise into 4, then halved

7½ cups fresh spinach leaves, tough stalks removed

2 large garlic cloves, crushed

8 oz/225 g canned cannellini beans, drained and rinsed

2 tsp dried oregano

4 tbsp half-fat sour cream

salt and pepper

One serving contains:
Energy kCal 277.31
Protein g 16.84
Carbohydrate g 38.51
Sugars g 11.01 **Fat g** 9.26
Saturates g 1.64
Fiber g 11.23
Sodium g 0.44

Preparation time 20 minutes

Cooking time 25 minutes **Serves 4**

1 Preheat the oven to 400°F/200°C. Place 4 pieces of foil on a counter and brush with oil. Place 2 mushrooms on top of one another on each piece. Brush the mushroom tops with oil, season with salt and pepper, and add 1 tablespoon of water. Fold the foil to make a package.

2 Place the packages on a baking sheet and bake for 20–25 minutes until the mushrooms are tender.

3 Meanwhile, steam the zucchini and spinach for 2–3 minutes until tender. Keep warm. Heat the oil in a heavy-bottom pan and add the garlic, beans, and oregano. Cook over medium-low heat for 2 minutes. Add the sour cream and heat through. Place the mixture in a blender and purée until smooth. Season with salt and pepper.

4 To serve, place a mushroom on each plate, top with a slice of zucchini, a spoonful of spinach, and the bean purée. Add the remaining zucchini and spinach, and top with a mushroom.

lasagna with roasted vegetables

This lasagna dispenses with the rich, high calorie béchamel and meat sauces.

2 tbsp extra virgin olive oil

1 tbsp balsamic vinegar

2 fresh rosemary sprigs

2 red bell peppers, seeded and quartered

2 zucchini, sliced lengthwise

2 red onions, peeled and each cut into 8 wedges

1 fennel bulb, sliced into thin wedges

8 vine-ripened tomatoes

1 head of garlic, unpeeled and top sliced off

16 black olives

8 sheets of dried lasagna

salt and pepper

shavings of fresh Parmesan cheese, to serve (optional)

PESTO DRESSING

1½ tbsp good quality pesto

1 tbsp olive oil

1 tbsp hot water

One serving contains:
Energy kCal 359.11
Protein g 8.44
Carbohydrate g 45.23
Sugars g 13.61 **Fat g** 18.29
Saturates g 1.65
Fiber g 7.85
Sodium g 0.32

Preparation time 20 minutes, plus 1 hour marinating

Cooking time 40 minutes **Serves 4**

1 Mix together the olive oil, vinegar, and rosemary in a large shallow dish. Place the red bell peppers, zucchini, red onions, fennel, tomatoes, and garlic in the dish and toss them in this mixture. Let marinate for at least 1 hour.

2 Preheat the oven to 400°F/200°C. Place all the vegetables except the tomatoes in a roasting pan with the marinade. Roast for 25 minutes, then remove the rosemary and garlic. Add the tomatoes and olives, then return to the oven and cook for an additional 15 minutes or until the vegetables are tender.

3 Meanwhile, squeeze out the soft roasted garlic from each clove, mash with a fork, and set aside. Mix together the ingredients for the pesto dressing. Cook the sheets of lasagna in plenty of salted boiling water following the package instructions, then drain.

4 To serve, place a sheet of lasagna on each plate and top with the roasted vegetables and garlic purée. Place another sheet of lasagna on top and add the pesto dressing and Parmesan, if liked.

teriyaki tofu and vegetable stir-fry

Tofu is a nutritious, lowfat ingredient made from soybeans. Its mild flavor means that it is best marinated before cooking.

3 tbsp teriyaki sauce

1 tbsp hot water

9 oz/250 g tofu, dried on paper towels and cut into cubes

1 tbsp peanut or vegetable oil

splash of toasted sesame oil

12 oz/350 g broccoli florets

6 oz/175 g fine green beans, trimmed

3 scallions, sliced on the diagonal

4 bok choy, sliced in half

2 garlic cloves, chopped

1 inch/2.5 cm piece of fresh gingerroot, peeled and finely chopped

6 tbsp fresh apple juice

4 tsp soy sauce

fresh cilantro leaves, to garnish

Preparation time 15 minutes, plus 1 hour marinating
Cooking time 20 minutes **Serves 4**

1 Place the teriyaki sauce and water in a shallow dish. Add the tofu and carefully turn it in the sauce until coated. Cover with plastic wrap and let marinate in the refrigerator for at least 1 hour.

2 Preheat the oven to 400°F/200°C. Place the tofu and marinade in a roasting pan and cook for 20 minutes, turning occasionally, until slightly crisp and golden on the outside.

3 Meanwhile, heat a skillet or wok and add both the peanut and sesame oils. Add the broccoli and green beans, then stir-fry, tossing the vegetables constantly, for 5 minutes.

4 Add the scallions, bok choy, garlic, and ginger and stir-fry for an additional 1 minute. Pour in the apple juice and soy sauce and cook for 1–2 minutes, adding a little extra water if the stir-fry appears dry.

5 Divide the stir-fry between 4 shallow bowls and top with the tofu. Garnish with cilantro just before serving.

One serving contains:
Energy kCal 333.37
Protein g 29.21
Carbohydrate g 36.36
Sugars g 13.71 **Fat g** 13.48
Saturates g 1.80
Fiber g 13.99
Sodium g 1.70

5 beyond dieting

For most people, the hardest part of weight control is not losing weight but keeping it off. However, it is possible, as long as you believe that you can control your weight, and combine sensible eating habits with a regular exercise regime. If you go back to your old habits you'll just put the weight back on and continue to gain. This is the main problem with crash diets—they don't help you make lifestyle changes that you can keep up in the long term.

Successful slimmers are those who've not only lost weight but managed to keep it off for good. They support themselves by selfmonitoring to stay conscious of their habits, whether it's through ongoing calorie awareness or keeping an occasional food diary. In this section, you'll find strategies to help you cope with those scenarios that throw you into nutritional chaos. Stay positive, congratulate yourself on what you've achieved so far, and believe in yourself. You can control your weight for life.

damage limitation

Just when you feel you're looking great, completely in control of your eating habits, and have plenty of energy to spare, life hits you with a crisis or obstacle, and all your good intentions disappear along with a large carton of ice cream. Then you start to feel annoyed with yourself, can't be bothered to exercise, and, even worse, feel that you've let yourself down. Don't despair, read through the following pages to identify which scenarios you're vulnerable to and learn how to deal with those diet saboteurs. Forewarned is forearmed!

Planning

Planning is essential if you want to maintain your svelte shape. Write down possible barriers to achieving your goal and strategies to overcome these. Plan your weekly meals, stock your refrigerator and pantry with healthy snacks and cook ahead if you can so you've always got something healthy and nutritious in the freezer. Planning also involves scheduling exercise (this will make you much more likely to do it), booking time for yourself (a great way to deal with stress), and being aware of when you're entertaining or eating out so that you can adopt the appropriate strategies.

Food and activity diary

This is one of the biggest guns in your arsenal to deploy in the war against excess weight. Keep a food and activity diary for a week or so before you even embark on your weight loss program to observe your habits and identify problem areas (see pages 110–111 for an example). Many of us reach for the cookie jar when we're bored. Anticipate this by writing down the times of the day (or week or month) when you're vulnerable to uncontrolled grazing, then plan a list of activities to do to stop yourself. Keep up the diary during your diet and beyond to keep track of what you're eating—people who do, keep the weight off.

▲ **Write it down**
Monitor your eating and activity habits by keeping a diary.

▶ **Shop sensibly**
Make a list of healthy food in advance—and stick to it!

HOW TO BE A
SUCCESSFUL SLIMMER FOR LIFE

1 Check your weight regularly (but no more than once a week) or assess how your clothes fit.

2 Don't ban any foods, but do limit the amount of those you know will pile on the pounds. This won't do the rest of your family any harm either.

3 Don't reprimand yourself if you overeat.

4 Address and confront problems rather than trying to eat, drink, smoke, sleep, or just wish them away.

5 Continue to eat a balanced diet with plenty of fruit and vegetables.

6 Eat regular meals at regular times.

7 Sit down to eat your meals, take time over them, and pay attention to what you're eating.

Shopping

Never go shopping when you're hungry—you'll end up with a cart of junk food and nothing nutritious to eat. Always make a list and stick to it. Even better, shop online. You don't have to face the temptation of the cookie aisle and the money you spend on delivery charges will be canceled out by the impulse buys you didn't make.

coping with cravings

By learning to cope with cravings you can stay firmly on track for weight control. Hunger is only one of the reasons why we eat—stress, boredom, a social occasion, loneliness, the smell of food, or pure habit are all triggers. Triggers become so automatic that sometimes it really does seem that you can't control what you eat. For those who struggle with their weight, eating when you aren't really hungry is one of the biggest problems.

Taking charge

Cravings are a perfectly normal response to life and its demands and the good news is that you can control them. How we think affects how we respond to cravings. For example, on a bad morning you may crave a hamburger for lunch, but you still have time to decide whether to give in to the craving or not. Even after buying the food, you can still decide not to eat it. When deliberating, try this: think about the consequences if you eat it, how will you feel physically, and how will you feel about yourself? Fat? Slightly sick? Angry? If you don't eat it, how will you feel? Virtuous? In control? Thinner? Now think hard about how you would prefer to feel. Making a conscious decision like this helps you to feel in control of what you eat and to overcome those cravings.

TOP TIPS FOR DEALING WITH CRAVINGS

1 Never forbid a food—you'll only want it more.

2 Don't leave trigger foods in sight or easy reach.

3 Make yourself a star chart. Every time you resist a craving, award yourself a gold star. When you've got ten, buy yourself a small treat (not food-related!)

4 Most cravings will go away after about 20 minutes, so try to outlast them. Lock yourself in the bathroom and have a long soak, or go for a walk.

▲ **Treat yourself**
Avoid cravings by taking a long, relaxing bath.

eating out

Long-term weight management doesn't mean you can't ever go out and have a good time, so here are some creative ideas to help you keep control of what's on your plate.

Anticipate

If you know you've got an event coming up, try eating a little less the day before. If you can, plan what you are going to eat before you go out so that you're not tempted to over order.

Don't clear your plate

You don't have to eat everything that's put in front of you, particularly if you are in a restaurant. Your mother is not there to scold you for not clearing the plate (or if she is, remember it's your business, not hers, as to what you eat!).

Two not three

How many times have you eaten an appetizer, main course, and dessert only to find yourself feeling uncomfortably full? Skip the appetizer or dessert, and avoid the bread basket. You'll save money, too.

Buffet management

Buffet meals can spell disaster. The trick is to load your plate with the low-calorie options—the vegetables and salads—before finding room for the bread and food smothered in mayonnaise. Practice portion control, and eat the low-calorie foods first.

▼ **Choose light**
Order a light meal when you go out to a restaurant to eat.

new partner

Too many romantic meals washed down with a bottle of wine will play havoc with your waistline. The solution is to keep your romantic meals to a weekly treat, and not be tempted to eat the same amount as your partner—he or she can fill up on extra rice, vegetables, or potatoes if they wish. Everyone's metabolism is different, and it's also a sad fact of life that men need more calories than women, which is why men can get away with eating what seems to be twice as much as women without putting on an ounce.

alcohol

Alcohol is fine in moderation but there are two main reasons why it can sabotage weight control. Firstly, it's an appetite stimulant and secondly, it relaxes your inhibitions so you're more likely to be careless over what you eat. Never drink on an empty stomach—if you know you're going out drinking, eat something light before you go and position yourself well way from the nuts and potato chips lined up on the bar (they've probably been coughed over or dipped into by someone whose hands aren't as clean as yours anyway!). Alcohol is full of empty calories and the more you have, the more you want. You're better off limiting your intake to a couple of glasses two or three times a week and you'll appreciate it more, rather than drinking out of habit. Always start an evening out with a soft drink or glass of water and match every alcoholic drink with a nonalcoholic one. That way you're more likely not to binge, and you'll prevent the worst effects of a hangover by staying hydrated.

BACK ON TRACK
How to get your eating back under control when you've overdone it.

1 Phone a friend, family member, contact a slimming club, or log on to an online chatroom—whatever suits you. Finding support quickly is essential. Talk about the feelings that may be causing you to overeat. Be honest about what you're eating and actively plan to get yourself motivated again.

2 Get moving. Don't punish yourself with a 3-hour stint at the gym, but go for a long walk. This will work out your mind and body and help relax you.

3 Write it down. Look at your food diary, write down positive statements, and repeat them to yourself. Take responsibility for getting back on track. Look to the long term, think where you want to be this time next year and don't let anything stand in your way.

4 Stay positive and don't get discouraged by weight gain. It doesn't mean you've blown your weight loss strategy for good. Accept the setbacks and start again now.

5 Don't deprive yourself. Focus instead on what you're going to eat rather than what you're not going to eat.

◀ **Dinner for two**
Make healthy food a regular part of your romantic meals.

starting a new job

Whether you're racking up the hours in an attempt to impress or just getting to grips with the workload/commute, this is a prime time for takeouts, missed meals, and frequent blasts of caffeine washed down with whole milk. One solution is to cook in bulk on your day off so that you've got a stocked freezer and can put something nutritious in the microwave when you come home. Keep a bowl of fruit on your desk at work to give you vital bursts of energy when you need it, and always have a bottle of water on hand. A glass of water is a far better way to combat a midafternoon energy slump than another cup of coffee.

Living on your own

It's all too easy to fall into a routine of living off microwavable meals for one when you're single. It doesn't have to be this way, however. With a little planning, you can eat well every day of the week and keep your weight under control.

1 Write down a meal planner for the next two weeks, and ensure you have a balanced diet. Refer to the meal program on page 28 for inspiration.

2 Buy your fruit and vegetables loose. This way, you can buy the amounts you anticipate you'll consume and you won't end up with packs of rotting salad greens lurking at the bottom of the refrigerator.

3 Avoid the supermarket specials and the "buy one get one free" offers. Buying in bulk usually results in eating in bulk. However, it does make economic sense to buy multipacks of meat or fish and then bag up individual portions to store in the freezer.

4 Eating alone shouldn't be a joyless affair. Sit down at the table and take time to enjoy your food. You can even light candles and play some background music to enhance the experience.

▼ **Satisfying snacks**
Keep a bowl of fruit to hand to stave off energy slumps.

having young children

Who can resist the lure of a lukewarm fish stick lingering in a pool of ketchup? You'd never dream of ordering it in a restaurant, but when it's left on junior's plate... The key solution here is to remember that you are not a trash can! It's a hard habit to break, but don't eat the leftovers. Clear the plates straight away and put the leftovers in the trash can. Having children in the house often means a ready supply of potato chips, cookies, cakes, and candies. Keep these products out of your sight, and set a good example by snacking on fruit. This will encourage your children to do the same.

WHAT TO DO WHEN YOU HIT A WEIGHT PLATEAU

1 Try a new exercise routine: variety is the spice of life.

2 Try some new recipes.

3 Pamper yourself and schedule in some treats (make them nonfood ones).

4 Dejunk your wardrobe. Throw out anything shapeless, baggy, and dowdy—anything that reminds you of the shape you don't want to be.

5 Go shopping and buy some sexy new underwear.

6 Recognize your achievements—tell your friends how much weight you've lost and accept their compliments.

Tied to the kitchen

This is another hazard of having young children. On the whole, young children tend to eat when they're hungry, which means little and often. It's fine for them, but can be disastrous for you. Even if you've got your children trained to the point that they'll happily tuck into a bowl of hummus and carrot sticks, you'll find yourself salivating and before you know it, you're joining in and eating most of what's on the table, regardless of whether you're hungry or not. Here's how to limit the damage:

1 If you can't stop yourself from joining in, cut up an apple into small pieces, put it on a plate and sit down and eat with the children.

2 Make it a rule never to eat standing up and always to eat off a plate. You'll be surprised how much grazing this will stop.

3 Tape a list of your weight maintenance goals to the refrigerator.

4 Think beyond baking. Remember that you are a role model for your children and that it's good for them to help you make things other than cookies. Little ones can help you stir up fruit smoothies just as well as cakes.

time of the month

Many women find that no matter how hard they try, it's almost impossible to control food cravings when they're premenstrual, and this is when binging becomes a real temptation. Take comfort from the fact that your metabolic rate increases by about 140 calories a day in the two weeks leading up to your period, so you do actually need to eat a bit more, but not necessarily more chocolate! Try the following solutions:

1 When you feel food cravings beginning to take hold, reach for low-calorie snacks such as sticks of celery, vegetables, or pieces of fruit.

2 Keep a stock of healthy snacks to hand—small pots of yogurt, mini boxes of raisins, rice cakes, and small bananas, for example.

3 Some people swear by sniffing vanilla extract—and since satiety is linked to smell, it's certainly worth a try.

4 Brush your teeth after every meal—this can stop eating between meals in its tracks.

BREAKFAST: A SIMPLE WAY TO CONTROL YOUR FOOD INTAKE

Eating breakfast can help reduce snacking and avoid overeating later. Scientific evidence shows that the majority of breakfast eaters weigh less than those who skip breakfast. The most satisfying breakfasts work in two ways. They rapidly raise blood sugar levels for a quick burst of energy, which is followed by a longer term energy boost from complex carbohydrate, protein-containing foods that are more slowly digested. If you feel you've no time at home, make yourself a packed breakfast to eat on the train or at your desk—put in a granola bar, a handful of nuts, or a hard-cooked egg (make a batch one evening) and some fresh fruit. You don't have to eat breakfast at the crack of dawn—as long as you eat within several hours of waking up you'll be fine. If you've been skipping breakfast, try a few grapes or a plain oatcake. After a few days your body may feel like something more substantial.

Let down by weekends

You find it easy to stay in control all week, but somehow when Friday night comes, it's hard to be so stringent. The solution lies in planning ahead—if you know the weekend's going to be nonstop party action, eat 300 calories less the day before and plan to fit in some exercise over the weekend, even if it's just a long walk on Sunday. You could also try eating two meals instead of three on Saturday and Sunday. At the weekends, breakfast often segues into lunchtime, so why not have a healthy midmorning brunch and skip lunch altogether?

▲ Soothe your mood

Fruit will sustain your energy levels and
balance out mood swings by avoiding
stressful sugar surges.

MORE WAYS TO KEEP MOVING

Keeping the weight off isn't just about
watching what you eat, it's also about keeping
active. Try these easy options to get you moving:

HOME IMPROVEMENT ACTIVITIES

Decorating will give you a decent activity boost and help you
tick things off your to-do list as well.

PLAY WITH YOUR CHILDREN

Young children never seem to sit still, so go and play with them.
Not only is it great for bonding, you'll also feel the benefits after
half an hour of chasing round the park.

IN THE KITCHEN

Do a few bends and stretches by the sink (pretend
you're a ballerina at the barre) or dance around
the kitchen while you're waiting for the tea
kettle to boil.

crises

Bereavement, bad news, and family illness are prime times for losing your appetite or comfort eating. Remember that things will eventually settle down and don't be too hard on yourself if your eating habits slip. Remember to keep an eye on the long term.

Stress

This is something that is increasingly with us and it's all too easy to reach for food to make yourself feel better. Stress or new situations can throw the most dedicated dieter, but it doesn't have to mean doom. The main trick is to build regular slots into your life where you actively do something to relieve stress, such as having a beauty treatment, going for a long walk in the country, gardening, or getting creative and painting a picture. Think of as many as 20 things that make you feel good and build them into your life. When you feel good about yourself, you'll think and act in a more positive way. Make sure you nourish your soul, not just your body.

ARMCHAIR AEROBICS
A workout without leaving your chair!
1 Buttock clenching. This can be done any time, anywhere. Just clench the muscles in your buttocks. Hold for a count of five, then slowly relax.
2 Arm circles (great for getting rid of "bat wing" arms). Sit up straight with your arms out to the side, palms upward. Slowly make circles with your hands.
3 Bust toner. Sit up straight and put your hands together as if you were praying. Then push your palms together as hard as you can. Count to ten and repeat five times.
4 Ankle circles. Gently circle your feet and ankles 20 times on each foot, then stretch out your leg and point your toes forward and backward ten times to work the calf muscles.

Traveling

Traveling in all its forms, from long car or train trips to flying off to exotic foreign climes, can present a real challenge for weight maintenance. Again, the trick here is to be prepared. Take a bottle of water and a packed lunch full of healthy eating options to eat on the way. You really don't want to stock up from the railway buffet or at the interstate service area. If you're flying, preorder a meal— most airlines have a wide range of special meals you can order, including vegetarian, lowfat, or low cholesterol. Just remember to forego any predinner drinks or nibbles on offer.

◀ **Family fun**
Playing with your children keeps you fit and is great for bonding.

nutrition and fitness diaries

Use these templates to create personal nutrition and fitness diaries that will help you to set yourself realistic goals and keep track of your progress. The comments and progress columns can be used to record motivation and energy levels, as well as achievement.

DATE	COMMENTS
breakfast	
lunch	
dinner	
snacks	
water	
other drinks	

1 monthly goal

2 weekly goal

3 daily goal

DATE

aerobic exercise	time	reps	other exercise	time	reps	progress

index

A

activity diary 98, 111
alcohol 23, 103
antioxidants 21
arm exercises 44–5, 109
attitude 8–9, 40–1, 109

B

binges 100, 103, 106, 109
Body Mass Index (BMI) 7
breakfast 20, 26, 29, 106
breathing 40–1
buttock exercises 49, 109

C

caffeine 23, 104
calories required 13
carbohydrates 12–13, 18–19, 27
chest 44–5, 109
children 105, 108
cholesterol 20, 36, 37
clothing 39
comfort eating 16–18
cravings 16, 18, 100, 106
crises 109

D

diets
  14-day plan 24–33
  failure 8, 97, 103
  optimum nutrition 19–21
  popular 12–14
drinks 19, 22–3, 44, 56–9, 103

E

eating out 101
eating patterns 6, 16–18, 25–7, 99, 103, 104–6
exercise 6, 34–51, 98, 103, 108–9, 111

F

facial workout 50–1
fats 13–14, 16, 20
fish, oily 20
fish recipes 83–9
food combining diets 13
food diary 98, 103, 110
food intolerance 12, 29, 55
fruit 19, 21, 22, 104
fruit juice 19, 21, 56

G

goals 8, 11, 98

H

height, and weight 14–15
hip exercises 49

J

juices 19, 21, 56

L

leg exercises 48–9, 109
low calorie diets 13
low-carbohydrate diets 12
lowfat diets 13–14
lower body exercises 48–9

M

macronutrients 19–20
meal times 26, 99, 106
meat recipes 74–81
menopause 16
metabolic rate 13, 14, 16, 35, 106
micronutrients 20–1
minerals 12, 21
motivation 8–9, 40–1, 97, 103

N

nutrition 16–21
nuts 20, 21, 26, 27

P

partner, new 103
planning 26, 37, 98, 101, 103, 106, 109
points systems 14
posture 38
poultry recipes 74–81
premenstrual days 106
proteins 12, 13, 19–20

R

recipes
  drinks 56–9
  fish 82–9
  meat and poultry 74–81
  salads 66–73
  soups 60–5
  vegetarian 90–5

S

safety 37, 47
salads 66–73
shopping 27, 99, 104
shoulders 44–5
skin care 52–3
smoothies 59
snacking 26, 27, 98, 106
soups 60–5
stomach exercises 46–7
stress 16, 35, 109
stretching 42–3

T

traveling 109

U

upper body exercise 44–5

V

vegetables 20, 21, 26, 27
vegetarian recipes 90–5
vitamins 12, 20–1

W

waist 7, 46–7
water 22, 44, 104
weekends 106
weight guides 7, 15
weight loss
  goals 8, 11, 98
  keeping it off 96–111
  plateau 105
work 104